"Bravo, Michael Connolly and Brie Goolbis! The remarkable stories of youth making the world a better place through their creativity and innovation left me with the distinct impression that the future can be brighter for future generations. When I read this book, I couldn't help but think of David Bornstein's, *How to Change the World: Social Entrepreneurship and the Power of New Ideas*, in which he explains, 'People who solve problems must somehow first arrive at the belief that they *can* solve problems. This belief does not emerge suddenly. The capacity to cause change grows in an individual over time as small-scale efforts lead gradually to larger ones. But the process needs a beginning—a story, an example, an early taste of success— something along the way that helps a person form the belief that it is possible to make the world a better place. Those who act on that belief spread it to others. They are highly contagious. Their stories must be told.' Thank you both for telling these stories!"

> ~ **Curtis L. DeBerg, Ph.D.**, Founder of Students for the Advancement of Global Entrepreneurship [SAGE]; author of *How High Is Up?*; Professor, California State University, Chico.

"Young Enough To Change the World is a collection of inspiring stories of compassionate and motivated young people who overcame huge obstacles to realize their dreams of helping others less fortunate than themselves. It is a 'must read' for those involved in mentoring students to create and sustain community service projects. The young people whose stories fill this book are truly inspiring. They are not our future leaders; they *are* our leaders."

> ~ **Bill Oldread**, Assistant Director, *EARCOS* (East Asia Regional Council of Schools).

"The timing of this book couldn't be better since society is at a tipping point with concerns for the younger generation who exhibit narcissistic behaviors and an assumption of entitlement. The 'can-do' attitude of these avant-garde innovators will renew our faith in young people who show us first-hand how to make this world a better place. I plan to showcase this book in my 'Mindset and Grit' workshops as a prime example of the deeds of *gritty* trailblazers who have given us hope for the future with their perseverance and courage."

> ~ **Jim Grant**, author of *If You're Riding a Horse and It Dies, Get Off*, Grit Consultant and Founder of Staff Development for Educators.

"*Young Enough to Change the World* offers a fresh, optimistic view of what can happen when kids and teens are given a chance to take an authentic role in changing their world. Those who argue for more autonomy, competency, and relatedness in school curriculums will cheer the accounts of students, who under the guidance of perceptive adult advocates have made remarkable contributions to society. The authors take the reader on a journey around the globe with inspiring stories of young people who have made a commitment to serving needs larger than their individual desires. Simply written and beautifully told, these stories address the importance of trusting students to perform selfless acts for no other reason than *it's the right thing to do.*"

> ~ **Debbie Silver, Ed.D.**, speaker, humorist, award-winning teacher and best-selling author of *Drumming to the Beat of Different Marchers; Finding the Rhythms for Differentiated Learning; Fall Down 7 Times, Get Up 8: Teaching Kids to Succeed;* and *Deliberate Optimism: Reclaiming the Joy in Education.*

young enough
TO
CHANGE
THE
WORLD

young enough TO CHANGE THE WORLD

**STORIES OF KIDS AND TEENS WHO
TURNED THEIR DREAMS INTO ACTION**

Michael P. Connolly and Brie K. Goolbis

KALINDI PRESS
Chino Valley, AZ

Cover design: Adi Zuccarello
Cover image by Georgina Quintana, *Sprout*, Oil on wood, 2004.
Interior design and layout: Becky Fulker, Kubera Book Design, Prescott, AZ

Library of Congress Cataloging-in-Publication Data
Connolly, Michael R.
 Young enough to change the world : stories of kids and teens who turned their dreams into action / Michael R. Connolly and Brie K. Goolbis.
 pages cm
 Includes bibliographical references.
 ISBN 978-1-935826-38-5
1. Youth--Political activity--Case studies--Juvenile literature. 2. Young volunteers--Case studies--Juvenile literature. 3. Social action--Case studies--Juvenile literature. 4. Voluntarism--Case studies--Juvenile literature. 5. Humanitarianism--Case studies--Juvenile literature. 6. Social entrepreneurship--Case studies--Juvenile literature. I. Goolbis, Brie K. II. Title.
 HQ799.2.P6C663 2015
 361.20835--dc23
 2014042561

Kalindi Press
PO Box 4410
Chino Valley, AZ 86323
800-381-2700
www.hohmpress.com

This book was printed in the U.S.A. on recycled, acid-free paper using soy ink.

the Seeker's Story

Past the seeker as he prayed,
came the sick, the hungry, the poor and tired and forsaken.
And in anguish the seeker cried out,
"Oh, dear God, how can you look upon such misery
and not do something?"
And deep down in the depth of his soul, the seeker heard a voice:
"I *did* do something; I made *you*."

Contents

PART III THE STUDENTS AND THEIR MENTORS

Preface

Many young people today long to make a positive difference in the world, not just when they have grown up, but even while they are still young. Presented with an opportunity and support, they have the ability to do that. Alexander the Great, Joan of Arc, Mary Shelley, (author of *Frankenstein*) and Louis Braille (who created the Braille system), all made a major contribution to society before they were out of their teens.

So what is keeping young people from realizing their dreams of making a difference, of leaving their mark on our world? John Gardner's book, *Self-Renewal* is about the need for societies to periodically renew themselves; it offers an explanation that all of us would do well to reflect upon. He wrote, "We have designed our society in such a way that most of the possibilities open to the young today are either bookish or frivolous." Instead of complaining about young people and how they are so absorbed in themselves and their technological toys or how they are not performing well in school, perhaps it's time we invited them to participate in what Gardner called "the great tasks of our times" and see how they respond.

Our experiences working as educators in schools both in the United States and around the world is that most kids and teens respond enthusiastically, even heroically, when given an invitation to work on a project designed to enhance the lives of others. Indeed, many don't even wait for an invitation, but act on their own when they see a need. Yet there is much more to be accomplished to address the great tasks of our times and many more young people need to be summoned to take up the challenge.

The young people whose stories we chronicle in this book do not regard themselves as heroes; Dylan Mahalingam even expressed concern when we told him we were going to use that term to describe him. He and the others in this book maintain that they are just "ordinary" young people who have seen a need and are determined to do something about it. Nonetheless, we believe they are heroes and deserve to be recognized.

The word *hero* comes from the Greek meaning, "to serve and protect." To the Greeks, a hero was someone who was willing to sacrifice his or her needs or comfort for the greater good of others. Self-sacrifice thus is a defining characteristic of all heroes, which certainly makes the kids and teens chronicled in this book heroes.

These young people from around the world possess another characteristic of ancient and modern heroes—*enthusiasm*. That is also a word that comes to us from the Greeks. *En theos* literally means "god-inspired." Every major religion relates a message that the road to personal salvation lies in a person's willingness to help others who are less fortunate. While none of the heroes in our book specifically mention their religious convictions, it's impossible to miss the spiritual roots that lie beneath what they have chosen to do. Their work is truly spirit-inspired.

In publishing the stories of these young heroes, we hope to accomplish at least two things. First, we hope that young people who read this book will be inspired to break the bonds of their own disempowerment and find ways to make their schools, their neighborhoods, their country and the world better. Indeed, their efforts don't have to be on a grand scale to make a profound difference in the lives of others. As you will see, many of the heroes in these pages began with a very small project that grew and gained momentum and support from others in spite of its small beginning. The key to these heroes' success is their passion and determination.

Secondly, we hope that adults who read these pages will recognize the desire of young people to help build a just world and will encourage more of them to join in efforts to make our world a healthier, more peaceful, more equitable place for all of us. As you read through these stories, you will meet parents, neighbors and teachers who are already supporting the young people in their lives. You will come to know the joy and satisfaction they feel when they see the remarkable things inspired youngsters and adolescents are capable of accomplishing.

PART I

THE YOUNGSTERS

1

P.J.'S Pantry

When a poor person dies of hunger,
it has not happened because God did not take care of him or her.
It happened because neither you nor I
wanted to give that person what he or she needed.

~ Mother Teresa

Peighton Jones was by all accounts a typical nine year old when
we first spoke to her in June 2011. She was attending Grade
5 at Pauline South Elementary School in Topeka, Kansas.
Her favorite subjects were physical education and math. She
liked to fish (catch and release), to play in the yard on the
swings with her siblings and friends, and she liked to watch
cartoons. During that summer she took swimming and tennis lessons, as well as visited the library to get new reading material. Sometimes she could be seen climbing into the
family car to go shopping with her parents, another activity
that she found enjoyable. But in one respect Peighton was
not at all typical. She was and is remarkable for what she
has accomplished.

It was on one such shopping excursion when she was
seven that Peighton experienced a turning point in her life.
She has a depth of kindness that is unequalled in most
youngsters her age and even in many who are older. But
more than just having a big heart, Peighton is driven by

her compassion to perform acts of charity and service. It is this drive that was ignited while shopping with her parents that day.

Waiting at the front of the store with her father while her mother finished paying for groceries, Peighton played a little game of observing what was happening around her. She noticed a mother and her daughter begin the checkout process. It wasn't the individuals themselves, or what they purchased, or how much they purchased, that held Peighton's attention. What interested her was that when they had finished shopping and everything was rung up, all of a sudden the mother began to hand several of the items on the checkout counter back to the cashier. This, as Peighton knew, was not how things are done at a supermarket. She could not imagine what the woman was doing.

She did not say anything to her dad at that moment, but that evening it was Dad's turn to put her to bed. While preparing to say her prayers, Peighton asked her father why that woman at the store was giving things back to the cashier in the store. Her father explained to his daughter that the woman did not have enough money to pay for all of the items that she had planned to buy. A discussion followed about why some people have enough money to purchase what they need, while others do not; it was a discussion that most seven year olds would not be interested in having, never mind initiating. Peighton's young mind began to wonder about the little girl who would not get to enjoy the food that her mother had planned to buy that day.

At that very moment Peighton's mission began to take shape. "I wanted," she told us, "to help people who couldn't afford a lot of things." And so, she conceived an idea to help those who could not afford even the basic necessities of life. The concept was easy—let everybody in her neighborhood know that she was going to collect both food items and money as donations to help those in need. Thus began P.J.'s Pantry, as Peighton likes to call it.

You might wonder how Peighton, at seven, was even aware of food pantries. The answer is quite simple: she watched her parents regularly make donations to food drives at various locations around town. The concept of giving to those less fortunate was often discussed within the family as they made those charitable donations.

In October 2009 to stock her "pantry" for the very first time, Peighton sent out over three hundred copies of an appeal letter she had written. The letter began: "My name is Peighton and I'm in the second grade. I'm collecting cans of food for people who don't have enough to eat this winter." It then went on to explain what prompted her decision to collect food and that she and her dad would be coming around to collect donations. She walked around her community, delivering the letters to her neighbors and friends.

A few days later, accompanied by her father, she went around the neighborhood again pulling a little red wagon to collect contributions. She managed to gather over 400 food items, along with some money during her first few collection weekends. While at first a bit apprehensive about how many people might respond to her letter, Peighton quickly discovered how generous her neighbors were. "All but one person made a donation," she remembers.

So, how many cans or boxes of food can someone put into a red Radio Flyer wagon? The answer is, not enough. Several weekends and dozens of trips throughout the neighborhood

1.1: P.J. surrounded by donations, October 2010.

were required to transport all of the food items back to the family garage where they were stored for the short-term and from where they were transported to the Topeka Rescue Mission. Peighton was especially grateful to her parents, who assisted with the heavy lifting when the wagon got full.

We all know how short the attention span of a seven year old can be, but not so with this little girl. After the first year of P.J.'s Pantry, a routine evolved. Peighton began to set aside the autumn for P.J.'s Pantry collections. Two years later in October 2011, Peighton delivered more letters and collected over 1,100 items for her pantry. The following year over 1,200 food items were received as Peighton enlisted the assistance of her sister and two cousins. Now that she had the extra help, she hoped to double her bounty every year. She was already making plans to get additional community support from local stores in her area during her next yearly collection.

1.2: Peighton and donations two years later.

That was an expectation that would soon be reached, and then exceeded.

In 2013, Peighton collected over 6,600 food items for her pantry since her father's business and local stores began to enthusiastically support her work. In 2014, that number climbed to over 8,000 items.

When complimented on all that she has accomplished, Peighton is quick to point out that, "Anyone can do it! All they need is determination and a real commitment." Her advice to others is quite simple: "Go ahead and just do it. You can make a big difference in how many people are getting fed and clothed. It might just take a bit of help in getting started." Even with the commitment that she has made and all that she has done over the past several years, Peighton still says that she feels she can do more to help people. She says that it saddens her when she sees how little certain people have and that it has taught her not to take for granted the things she has. She is determined to do more to help families who don't have enough money to live on.

It truly is extraordinary to see someone so young recognize a problem and then follow through with an action plan to solve that problem. As the great Dr. Seuss once explained in *The Lorax*, "Unless someone like you cares a whole awful lot, nothing is going to get better. It's not." I wonder if Peighton ever read that book.

If you see a little girl with a blond ponytail hanging down her back walking by your house pulling a red Radio Flyer wagon, please go immediately to your cupboard to find a few food items to donate. Peighton will be immensely grateful, as will all those who go to the local food pantries in Topeka, Kansas to enjoy the bounty she has collected.

1.3: Peighton's bounty headed for the Topeka Rescue Mission in late 2014.

Peighton Jones has made a special effort on behalf of those less fortunate, and she has had a huge impact on making her town a place where all can find a hot meal when they need it. By being willing to donate her time, by mustering her energy and compassion, she has learned that the determination of one small girl can make a big difference in the lives of many.

Speaking of big, as Peighton's food collection totals continue to grow, don't be surprised if, in the future, you see a large truck following that little blonde girl and her wagon around the neighborhood.

2

Mini's Mission: Burn Rubber to Help Another

No one has yet fully realized the wealth of sympathy,
kindness and generosity hidden in the soul of a child.
The effort of every true education should be to unlock that treasure.
~ Emma Goldman

Like other kids, Timmy "Mini" Tyrrell enjoys having fun. Most Saturday nights from March through December he can be found at the racetrack. Timmy is a go-kart racer—and, from all reports, a very good one. He started racing at the Old Dominion Raceway in Virginia when he was four years old. That year he finished third in the Kid Kart I Series. He's a competitor and it doesn't take much to get his competitive spirit fired-up. The first day he was planning to race, he was told that he was too little. Taking that as a challenge, Timmy went home and practiced for hours every day. When he returned to the raceway, he won the next five races.

But Timmy Tyrrell is more than just a fun-loving competitive racer. He possesses the sympathy, kindness and generosity that Emma Goldman is speaking about—and he doesn't keep it hidden. His mother Tina says that even when he was two years old, Timmy would eagerly share

10

2.1 Eight-year-old "Mini" at the Capital City Speedway in Ashland, VA in 2012.

his toys with other kids. He was even willing to give his toys away when a local minister came collecting toys for disadvantaged children.

As a racecar driver, Timmy enjoys winning. But for him a race is much more than just a contest about who will finish first and win a trophy. Each lap actually represents a round in a much more important contest: the battle against childhood cancer.

"Mini" (the nickname he received because his father is also named Timmy), races to raise funds to find a cure for pediatric cancer. Friends, neighbors, relatives, classmates, teachers and even total strangers donate or pledge money for each lap he finishes or each race he enters. In one year alone, he raised over $30,000. Timmy was on a mission, and that mission was to help as many children suffering from cancer

2.2: "Mini" in the Victory Lane after winning First Place in that race!

as he could. Indeed, his goal has now become a challenge to actually eliminate childhood cancer entirely.

Of course, *Mini's Mission* didn't begin with the grandiose idea of raising thousands of dollars; it began modestly. It started when little Timmy's friend, let's call her Amy, was diagnosed with brain cancer. Timmy was six when he overheard Amy's parents talking about the symptoms of her cancer, which included loss of pituitary gland function, thyroid disease, adrenal insufficiency and damage to her hypothalamus. He didn't, of course, understand all the details of his friend's diagnosis, but, as he later told his Dad, "This isn't good."

As Amy's parents talked, Timmy heard about the many unforeseen costs that families of children with cancer face. Added to the expense of hospitalization, medicines, and doctors' care, there are the additional expenses of driving back and forth between the hospital and home. He learned that Amy's parents were struggling to keep up with their electrical and telephone bills, their house and car payments. After her parents left, Timmy said to his Dad, "Maybe I can find a way to help Amy and other sick children."

He and his Dad talked about the details. They decided that Timmy could use his racing as a fundraising activity. Thus was born the idea for *Mini's Mission*. Good fortune often follows good decisions. That's what happened. One day, Brandon Edwards, President of Inspired Athletes, Inc., an organization whose goal is to feature stories of people who encourage others to overcome adversity, came to one of Mini's races. He was impressed. He helped Timmy come up with a name for his mission, a name that captures the sound of a racetrack's squealing tires and smoking rubber—*Burn Rubber to Help Another*. Edwards also featured *Mini's Mission* on his Inspired Athletes website.

By the time *Mini's Mission* got up and running and donations started coming in, his friend Amy had completed her treatment. That could have brought an end to his project, yet it didn't, because Timmy asserts, "I don't like cancer." So he donated the funds he had raised to the Jeffrey Virostek Fund. Jeffrey was a boy who suffered from acute myelogenous leukemia and died when he was just four years old.

Once underway, *Mini's Mission*, like a racecar accelerating, began to pick up momentum. Brian Williams of NBC Nightly News became aware of Timmy's commitment to helping others and featured him in a segment of *Making A Difference*. Then one of Timmy's heroes, NASCAR driver Jeff Gordon, saw that news segment and invited Timmy to meet him at the Martinsville Speedway in Virginia. Jeff expressed admiration for Timmy and what he was doing. Gordon had established the Jeff Gordon Children's Foundation and was raising millions of dollars to support those battling childhood cancer and their families. He decided to match the $7,000 Timmy had recently raised. NBC Nightly News did a follow-up story on Timmy and Jeff and their mutual dedication to putting an end to childhood cancer.

By March 2012, *Mini's Mission* elected to team up with the Jeff Gordon Children's Foundation. It seemed a natural fit; two young men who love racing and who are also devoted to helping those less fortunate. By then, Timmy had become a celebrity in his own right—the face of the fight against childhood cancer. In addition to NBC Nightly News and CNN, a number of newspapers also featured him in their stories. Timmy now also has his own Facebook page with over 3,100 friends and his own website: www.minismission.com. He is also becoming an accomplished public speaker, frequently called upon to address elementary and high school as well as adult audiences to encourage them to join him in the fight against cancer.

For Mini, though, it's not about drawing attention to himself, it's about drawing attention to the struggles and getting support for those children battling cancer; ultimately it's about getting rid of childhood cancer entirely. "I want to throw cancer away and never have it come back," he explains.

Where does a child as young as Timmy acquire that spirit of compassion for others and the drive that turns that compassion into altruistic action? It might have always been a part of his personality, as his mother Tina suggests, but there is another little story that might in part explain where his empathy originated.

Timmy's Aunt Tara is a paraplegic confined to a wheelchair and she keeps an extra wheelchair in her house. When he was a toddler, Timmy would ride that wheelchair whenever their family visited. It became known as "Timmy's chair."

One night when Timmy was three years old, the family was home and Timmy's father saw a story on the local news about a college student who was suffering from spina bifida. The girl, who was only able to walk short distances, had gone to a Halloween house party and left her wheelchair outside by the door and someone had stolen it. Timmy's Dad, whom Tina describes as "the biggest softie there is," was so moved by the story he wanted to do something to help her.

He thought of Aunt Tara's spare wheelchair and spoke to Tina's sister about lending the girl that wheelchair until hers was returned. It was agreed, yet there was another matter that had to be addressed before they could follow through with their plan—this, after all, was "Timmy's chair." When his father and aunt talked to him about what they wanted to do, three-year-old Timmy readily agreed, "As long as she brings it back when she gets her chair back," he told them.

Emma Goldman is right: A lot of us have yet to realize the wealth of sympathy, kindness and generosity hidden in the soul of a child. When we see it in children like Timmy, we are often astonished, although we shouldn't be, because as Timmy says, "Anyone can make a difference if they find something they want to do and then go out and do it."

Timmy "Mini" Tyrrell is making a difference in the world and in the lives of children with cancer and their families. He is a positive role model for many people, young and old in his school, community, country and also around the world. His buddy, fellow racecar driver and now partner in fighting childhood cancer, Jeff Gordon, summed up what we must never forget, "Young kids like Timmy can inspire us all."

2.3: "Mini" in September 2014.

In September of 2014, "Mini" turned ten and entered the fifth grade. His enthusiasm for racing remains undiminished. He continues to race go-karts, but has also moved up to racing Arena Cars (half scale stock cars), at Richmond Indoor Coliseum and racing Bandoleros, another kind of miniature stock car, at Charlotte Motor Speedway and Atlanta Motor Speedway. Timmy has the distinction of being the youngest ever (at age nine) to race a full-sized late model stock car at the Shenandoah Speedway.

His friendship and partnership with Jeff Gordon has remained firm. For the past three years as part of the Jeff Gordon Children's Foundation/Kick-It.org, "Mini" has raised over $200,000 through tournaments and racing. In 2014, he raised another $15,000 for a Jeff Gordon Vital's Room at the Children's National Medical Center in Washington, DC. All who know him realize that he intends to win his biggest race—the race to find a cure for childhood cancer.

PART II

THE ADOLESCENTS

3

Lil' un Millennium Development Goals

*When you carry out acts of kindness, you get a wonderful feeling.
It is as though something inside your body responds and says,
yes, this is how I ought to feel.*
~ Harold Kushner

Sometimes a young hero's determination to improve the lives of others is ignited by an off-handed comment. "We could feed a poor family in another country for a week with the food that you leave on your plate," Dylan Mahalingam's mother would often tell him.

Dylan admits that at first, he wondered how he might find some way to ship the food he didn't want to eat to that poor family in another country. But then something happened that brought the reality of what his mother was saying home to him in a very heartbreaking way. "We went on a family trip to India and as we passed through cities and rural villages, I saw people begging for money and living in the streets. What shocked me most was seeing the children begging or working for a living in factories instead of going to school as they should have been," recalls Dylan.

That was when he recognized the sad truth behind what his mother had been telling him. Even though he was only eight years old at the time, Dylan decided that he had to do something to alleviate the suffering he had witnessed. But what was he to do? Where was he to start? Those were the questions that needed answers.

Fortunately, Dylan had a mentor close at hand. His older sister Ammu had been doing a lot of charity work—volunteering for HIV awareness programs and other projects. When Dylan expressed his desire to help eliminate some of the hardship he had witnessed in India and asked her for ideas about what he might do, she suggested he consider the recently adopted United Nations Millennium Development Goals.

A self-proclaimed "computer geek," eight-year-old Dylan easily located those goals online. When he read them, he knew he had his answer. He decided he would start a charitable foundation that would help advance those eight Millennium Development Goals adopted by the United Nations in September 2000:

1. Eradicate Extreme Hunger and Poverty
2. Achieve Universal Primary Education
3. Promote Gender Equality and Empower Women
4. Reduce Child Mortality
5. Improve Maternal Health
6. Combat HIV/AIDS, Malaria and Other Diseases
7. Ensure Environmental Sustainability
8. Develop a Global Partnership for Development

Still, there remained the question of where to begin. He contacted two of his cousins, Pooja Dharan, who lived in Maryland, and Courtney Fillerbrown from Massachusetts.

Together they discussed several ideas that eventually led them to establish the Lil' MDGs [The Little Millennium Development Goals] Foundation. Dylan was nine when the organization was officially launched in 2004, Pooja was seven and Courtney, eight. Dylan then began recruiting a few of his school friends to help.

The Lil' MDGs team first created a website for their new non-profit foundation. Youth Making Changes: http://lilmdgs.org/ [still active]. They knew that a lot of young people wanted to contribute to making the world better, yet they might not know how to go about doing it. The website creators were convinced that by using the power of the Internet and social media, they could educate young people about the social problems the Millennium Development Goals were designed to address and also show them ways that they could help further those goals. Dylan recognized that when young people are aware of a problem, their compassion is stirred and they want to help. After all, isn't that what happened to him when he had witnessed the poverty in India?

Dylan's small but growing team immediately encountered one of the major obstacles that young activists who undertake ambitious social projects inevitably confront—adult skepticism. Many grownups have a difficult time believing that committed young people, regardless of their age, can have an impact on our world. "The biggest challenge," Dylan recalls, "was getting adults in companies and other organizations to take us seriously because back then we were even younger than we are now."

The Indonesian tsunami that struck in December 2004 would help dispel adult skepticism about the influence of the Lil' MDGs. Working with other charitable organizations, the Lil' MDGs Foundation helped raise over $11,000,000. Dylan and his two cousins began their fundraising activities for tsunami relief by making jewelry and going door-to-door in their neighborhoods. Additionally, Dylan composed a letter requesting donations that his mother Krithika took to her workplace.

Yet, the most effective way of making people aware of the devastation the tsunami caused and of soliciting their help and contributions to relieve the misery it had produced, Dylan discovered, was by leveraging the power of the Internet and social media. He and four of his friends created a website entitled *Killer Waves* to educate young people about tsunamis and the havoc they inflict both on human beings and on nature. That website would eventually win its five creators first place in the 2005 ThinkQuest Internet Challenge.

Its enormous fundraising achievement during the Indonesian tsunami in 2004 marked the beginning of the Lil' MDGs success in establishing credibility as a humanitarian non-profit organization. The foundation gained added reliability when it was recognized by the Oracle Foundation, a non-profit educational organization. Oracle agreed to host their website, and as a result it became viewable around the world.

Recognition by Oracle didn't come by accident, however. Dylan's older sister and mentor Ammu was significant in bringing that relationship about. As Dylan's mother explains, her daughter had worked for the Oracle Foundation, travelling and speaking on behalf of its educational programs. Ammu connected Dylan with her former colleagues there and her brother did the rest. As a bright, engaging and articulate

3.1: Dylan speaking in Manchester, NH for one of Lil' MDGs
benefit events in 2009 when he was fourteen years old.

spokesperson for Lil' MDGs, his passion, commitment and conviction about the importance of young people working to accomplish the Millennium Development Goals was palpable. Oracle was impressed.

Once given worldwide exposure by Oracle, Lil' MDGs began to grow and its charitable work expanded significantly. It entered into a partnership with Jayme's Fund for Social Justice established by Caren Lipkin-Moore to honor the memory of her daughter Jayme who died tragically at the age of seventeen after being hit by a train. It was a natural partnership in a couple of ways. Like Dylan, Jayme was a passionate, young, social activist who championed the cause of human rights, tolerance, and quality education for all children. Coincidently, Jayme had been Dylan's babysitter.

From its modest beginning as the vision of three young people who wished to support those in need, Lil' MDGs has grown up to become a powerful force for improving the lives of marginalized people both in the United States and around the world. With more than 41,000 volunteers worldwide, the Lil' MDGs has unified the efforts of over 3,000,000 children in forty-four countries to make a tangible difference in the lives of over 1,000,000 people.

Recently as part of the Lil' MDGs commitment to raising awareness of social problems, a group of Lil' MDG volunteers in Turkey organized a flash mob street performance in which they dressed up as raindrops to educate passers-by about water scarcity in places like Africa. Another group of young volunteers walked barefoot around London to bring awareness to the struggles of young people in countries who must walk miles in bare feet to fetch water, or go to work on farms or in mines.

Making contact with socially committed young people around the globe is part of the Lil' MDGs model for success. Dylan establishes contacts through his work online, but also through his attendance at conferences dedicated to advancing the UN Millennium Development Goals, his participation on discussion panels, and through an ever-increasing number of speaking invitations.

The 2015 target date for achieving the United Nation's eight Millennium Goals—from halving extreme poverty to stopping the spread of HIV/AIDS—is rapidly approaching at the time of this writing. In order to meet that target, the Lil' MDGs Foundation believes that it has a crucial role to unlock the power of the Internet to educate, engage, inspire and empower youth in every corner of the world. While children everywhere are concerned about global issues, many still do not know how they can help. The passionate members, partners and 100% volunteer staff of the Lil' MDGs are dedicated to providing young people with opportunities to get involved.

Establishing partnerships with other humanitarian organizations is also an important component of the Lil' MDGs success. Working with non-governmental organization (NGO) partners like *Under the Acacia* in Africa; *Child Services* of Manchester, New Hampshire; *Jayme's Fund*; and *Generation On*, the Lil' MDGs has built a dormitory for a school in Tibet; a computer center, library, and a mobile hospital in India; a playground for a school serving AIDS orphans in Uganda; provided Christmas toys for needy children in the United States; books and learning supplies for children in Kenya; collected over 9,000 books for a library serving disadvantaged youth in Washington, DC; as well as supplying hurricane and tsunami relief in a variety of countries over the past ten years.

In 2011, Dylan and Lil MDGs, working with *Under the Acacia*, began a project to build a solar powered Internet kiosk in Loita Hills in Africa, home to over 150,000 members of the Maasai people. That work was completed a year later. The kiosk now provides the people of Loita Hills with online access, vocational training opportunities, and revenue for their community.

Despite all of the successes of the organization he helped create, and even after he has been personally recognized by Nestlé's Corporation as one of its Very Best Youth, having been invited to speak or participate on a variety of panels worldwide, including a recent United Nations Conference, as well as being featured as a speaker at a TEDx Teen event,

3.2: Dylan as a keynote speaker in 2012 for a Nestlé Foundation event in Los Angeles.

Dylan is an unassuming teenager, a regular guy. He loves to walk Nestle, his chocolate Labrador Retriever. (The name, he and his Mom insist, has no connection with the famous food company.) He enjoys the company of many friends and likes doing things that have nothing to do with the Lil' MDGs. Dylan has a wonderful sense of humor and loves to tell stories. Watch the YouTube video of his TEDx talk and hear him describe how his unsuccessful efforts to be master of his dog (she, he says, is *his* master) has led him to appreciate that we can't all be masters but we can all learn to serve others.

Throughout his high school years at Pinkerton Academy in Derry, New Hampshire, even with a demanding schedule working on the Lil' MDGs-related activities (including speaking engagements, participation on conference panels, and accepting awards for his service to others) that took him away from school on average once a month, Dylan was an honor student. He enjoyed all of his classes, but leaned particularly toward the sciences and technology.

Not surprisingly, in 2014, Dylan entered his sophomore year at Worcester Polytechnic Institute in Massachusetts, planning to major in Robotics Engineering. Dylan also has a black belt in karate, loves music and plays a number of musical instruments including piano, guitar, and ukulele. He enjoys tennis and basketball, swimming and snowboarding.

Although he continues to work for and speak on behalf of the Lil' MDGs, Dylan understands that his role as director of the foundation must someday come to an end. He has already prepared his successors to take a more active role in setting the future course of the organization. The success of the Internet kiosk project in Loita has led the group to consider expanding the initiative to other remote locations in Kenya.

For all that he has accomplished at such a young age, Dylan remains remarkably humble. When he talks about the awards he has received and the speaking invitations he frequently receives, he says that he does not view these as personal honors, but sees himself as a representative accepting the tributes on behalf of *everyone* in the Lil' MDGs organization. These awards and honors are, he also recognizes, opportunities to spread the organization's message and involve more young people in its work.

His mother says that when he heard us refer to him as a hero, he told her, "It's an honor that they think I'm a hero, but I want them to realize I'm just a normal teen. I don't want others to be thinking: I want to be like Dylan Mahalingam; that would be creepy. I want them to think that I'm just a normal boy. I want them to believe that if I can do it, others can too."

The simple yet powerful idea that Dylan wants other youngsters to accept is this: "No matter what it is, even if it is just a little thing, you can help. Every little bit that every person does can have a giant impact." His advice to young people is to find their passion and then pursue it. When he talks about the reward he gets from all his hours of hard work, his message resonates with the inspiring words of Harold Kushner. Dylan says, "Well, it sounds sort of cheesy to say it, but it is really true. When you help someone, you get this feeling inside that you did something, and it's just a really great feeling. Not only are you giving something, but you are also getting something back. So, it's sort of a mutual trade. The reality is that I'm benefitting as a person through this work."

Dylan Mahalingam has some advice for adults who may still be skeptical about a young person's ability to undertake a great humanitarian task. He says adults should believe in young people's capacity to make a difference, and if they need evidence, he says he has the statistical data that shows what child-led organizations around the world have accomplished. But, in truth, anyone looking for evidence of what dedicated young people on a mission can accomplish need look no further than Dylan and his Lil' UN Millennium Development Goals Foundation.

4

Free Movement: A Gift From the Heart

This is the true joy of life,
the being used for a purpose recognized by yourself as a mighty one;
the being a force of nature instead of a feverish,
selfish little clod of ailments and grievances
complaining that the world will not devote itself to making you happy.
~ George Bernard Shaw

Kunho Kim doesn't remember much about the accident that left him unconscious and paralyzed. He had gone skiing with friends in Great Falls, Montana where he was studying as an exchange student. He remembers that he attempted a ski jump that ended badly. Beyond that, he has no memory of what happened on that tragic day.

He does, however, vividly remember the conversation he had in the hospital with his mother and sister Stella who had flown from Korea to Montana when they heard of Kunho's accident. He recalls telling his mother that as a disabled person, he now faced very limited opportunities in life. His mother, however, did not agree.

"No," she told him. "Even though you can't walk, there are still lots of things you can do with your life." That comment, as well as what happened next, would convince Kunho that not only should he believe in his own undiminished potential, but that he could help other handicapped people to realize theirs as well.

An outpouring of support from friends, hospital staff, and other members of the Great Falls community where he was being treated immediately after the accident, would have a lasting effect on him. Nurses at Benefits Health Service bought him an Xbox to help him pass the time. School friends and other community members brought food and gift cards to help pay his sister's and mother's expenses while they were with him in the United States. A local Korean family even brought them Korean food.

It was, however, the lack of support he received from one sector that may have been the greatest influence on Kunho's decision to do what he ultimately decided to do once he was out of the hospital. The insurance company that was supposed to cover his medical expenses refused to pay for additional medical treatment if he remained in the United States. They insisted he return to Korea. "The insurance company in Sweden [that provided Kunho with health insurance during his year abroad] was absolutely bureaucratic and unsympathetic, and denied him a benefit he was entitled to," explained the Kim family's lawyer. So Kunho was forced to return to Korea.

When he was transferred to a hospital in Korea that specializes in spinal cord injuries, the kindness continued. Kunho remembers the doctors giving him copies of medical books because he wanted to learn more about his injuries and how they would be treated. He devoured those books and watched how the doctors supported him and other patients like him. "They did exactly what I had read in the books, he explains. Eventually he would return to Saigon South International School (SSIS) in Vietnam where he had been a student prior to going to the United States.

It was while he was still in the hospital, though, that a series of events transpired that would lead to his decision to create a charity that provides wheelchairs for paralyzed Vietnamese who cannot afford them. First, there was the insurance company's refusal to pay his medical expenses if he remained in an American hospital. Then there was the discovery that the wheelchair he would eventually need would cost $5,000. Finally, there was an email from a friend at the British International School in Saigon who wanted to know what he thought about a community action project she was considering—organizing a group of students to pick up litter in Saigon.

Kunho remembers that while he thought that was an admirable project, he also considered it pretty mundane. Everyone wants to do a project like that, he recalls thinking. It was then that he began to consider the people in Vietnam who had suffered injuries like his due to motorbike accidents or other mishaps. How many of them would be able to afford a wheelchair? His mother's conviction came to mind, that even though he couldn't walk, there was still much that he could actually accomplish in life. What if, like those people in Vietnam who couldn't afford a wheelchair, he was condemned to be in bed for the rest of his life? How much could he achieve then? A little voice inside told Kunho that he could do something about that—told him he *must* do something about that.

So he wrote back to his friend and asked her to investigate the number of spinal cord injuries in Vietnamese hospitals and how the patients were being treated. He knew that she had connections with hospital staff and could access that unclassified information. What his classmate reported back to him was not surprising, but it was disheartening. She told him that there were hundreds of patients with injuries like his, and that most of them were bedridden and couldn't afford a wheelchair.

"I had to stay in bed for two months after my injury and it was awful; I had bedsores and ulcers," Kunho remembers. "Hearing the news that you would have to stay in bed for your entire life would be devastating for most people," he explains. So he decided to do something to help those who were facing that kind of nightmarish life sentence. He asked friends to help him start a club that would donate wheelchairs to paralyzed Vietnamese patients. And so on July 9, 2010, four and a half months after his accident, HeartSays FreeMove was born.

HeartSays FreeMove, (a literal English translation from the Korean), is a non-profit international student volunteer group founded by Kunho and his friends Chang Duck Kim and Ida Yeo to raise awareness about spinal cord injury patients in Vietnam, the difficulties they face, as well as donate wheelchairs to those patients. Its slogan, "For every love, there is a heart to receive it," (a sentiment expressed by Ivan Panin) speaks to our human need to give and receive love.

Getting the HeartSays FreeMove Project off the ground was not a simple undertaking, however. There was the usual adult doubt about a grandiose student-initiated project to be overcome, as well as multiple bureaucratic hoops to jump through. Kunho recalls making a number of presentations to the Saigon South International School (SSIS) administration and faculty. He remembers recruiting students, encouraging them to join the venture, and then seeking a teacher advisor, all before the project could even get underway. But once these tasks were successfully completed, he and his group had permission to move on to the important task of fundraising. Although wheelchairs in Vietnam are a lot less state-of-the-art than Kunho's, and hence, a lot less expensive, they are still not cheap, costing about $100 each. In order to raise the kind of funds HeartSays FreeMove would need to make the sizeable wheelchair donations Kunho envisioned, his group couldn't just plan the typical student sponsored fundraisers like bake sales. So his friends wheeled him around to various companies and organizations where they could make their fundraising pitch.

They developed a PowerPoint presentation for their talk and passed out brochures describing the proposed project. Not surprisingly, certain CEO's expressed skepticism about the venture and its ability to positively impact the lives of paralyzed Vietnamese, but others complimented the students on their humanitarian work and made a donation. After listening to the students' presentation, the SSIS's PTA helped to further the project by making a sizeable donation of $3,000.

By November 2010, Kunho's group had made what he considered a modest donation of twelve wheelchairs to spinal cord injury patients in Vietnam. By March 2012, the number had risen to forty-seven newly mobile individuals who would otherwise have been confined to bed. Many of them are even currently able to work as a result of the gift of a wheelchair.

Despite the sudden and tragic accident that has changed his life in a way that many would consider heartbreaking,

4.1: Kunho in class in 2012.

Kunho doesn't view it that way. He sees being in a wheelchair as an unexpected blessing—one that has changed him in a very positive way. "Before the accident," he explains, "I used to be very tall and smart, and I looked down on people. Now that I am in a wheelchair, the perspective through which I see the world has changed a lot. I was actually seeing the world a little bit the wrong way. Now that I get help from so many people, I have the feeling that everyone is wonderful and caring. The world is bright and we have reason to hope."

Kunho admits that if he were not in a wheelchair, he'd probably be out playing soccer or basketball and engaging in a lot of other activities that kids his age do. He likely wouldn't have had much time or inclination to think about the things he is thinking about and doing now. For Kunho, being in a wheelchair is a blessing, in an ironic way, because it gives him the time to reflect on how he can help others less fortunate than he.

"At first," he says, when discussing his motivation for creating HeartSays FreeMove, "it was sort of like an obligation. I felt that I had to do something because when I was in the United States I got lots of support from people. I also felt I was very fortunate—I was able to have a special wheelchair because my parents could afford it. The difference between me and someone born in Vietnam was that I was born in Korea, a wealthy country. I didn't think that was fair."

Kunho soon moved from feelings of guilt to feelings of warmth and fulfillment once he began to see the influence his donations were having on the lives of the men and women in Vietnam who received the wheelchairs. Their smiles and their expressions of gratitude touched his heart and kept him going through challenging times as he and his student group worked to raise additional funds for more wheelchairs.

Every six months he and his student associates conducted a follow-up interview with the people who had received wheelchairs. Through students at SSIS who are Vietnamese, Kunho learned that the wheelchairs his group had donated have indeed profoundly changed the recipients' lives. They are not only grateful for the opportunity to be mobile, but also speak of how their new mobility has reduced stress in their families and allowed them, though handicapped, to resume work and feel more like normal human beings.

Before graduating from Saigon South International School, Kunho turned the management of HeartSays

FreeMove over to a new president and vice-president. The project continues to this day.

Like other young people whose stories are described in this book, Kunho has clearly heard that voice in the depth of his soul telling him that he can do something to relieve the suffering he sees in the world. He has responded to that voice and that has proven to be a good thing for him as well as those he has helped. When he talks about what others can do to make someone else's life better, he says, "Listen to your heart and do what your heart says you truly want to do. If you really believe that what you want to do can have an impact on people and can change the world, you can do it. If you have passion and keep on doing what you are doing, things will change sooner or later."

4.2: Kunho in San Francisco in 2014 during his research trip across the United States.

In May 2014, Kunho Kim completed his freshman year at Harvard University where he plans to major in Government and East Asian Studies. One of the many challenges he faced in his first year was negotiating the sidewalks of Harvard Square in Cambridge that he admits are not wheelchair-friendly. That led Kunho to embark on a new quest. When he had time away from his studies, he conducted a successful fundraising campaign for a summer vacation trip across the United States. That trip was not simply for pleasure. He is currently working on a travel friendly guide to American cities for wheelchair-bound people.

5

travelin' tunes

The power of music to integrate and cure...is quite fundamental.
It is the profoundest nonchemical medication.

~ Oliver Sacks

Sometimes a young hero's confrontation with the face of need can be very personal. As an infant, Samantha Fernandez was hospitalized with meningitis. Even after she was released from the hospital, she was still sickly and spent countless hours in her pediatrician's office. She recalls now how she liked to play with the stethoscope, blood pressure cuff and other medical paraphernalia she found there. She even keeps a picture of herself as a little girl dressed up in a doctor's outfit, complete with all the props.

It is not surprising then, to hear that Samantha wants to become a doctor—specifically a pediatrician. It is a bit surprising perhaps, to discover that as early as her first year in high school, she found her way into a hospital where she began to alleviate the pain and suffering of children through music.

Samantha has created a trio of young musicians: a singer, a keyboard player and guitarist, called Travelin' Tunes that visit Miami Children's Hospital each week and play for children with cancer and other serious illnesses or injuries. The trio travels from floor to floor and room to room offering to play for the kids.

5.1: Samantha assembling her cart at the hospital in 2010.

On a typical day, Samantha and her musical partners depart for the Children's Hospital at the end of their school day. Once there, Samantha checks a computer to find out how much time the hospital staff has allotted their trio for that day's musical tour. The three of them then assemble, clean and sanitize a cartful of instruments for the patients to play, including tambourines, small guitars, drums and maracas purchased with funds raised by Travelin' Tunes. The three young people then wheel the cart around, inviting the children to take an instrument to play and sing along. Once they have completed a tour of all three floors, the Travelin' Tunes musicians return the cart to its room, clean and sanitize the instruments again, and then head home to do their homework.

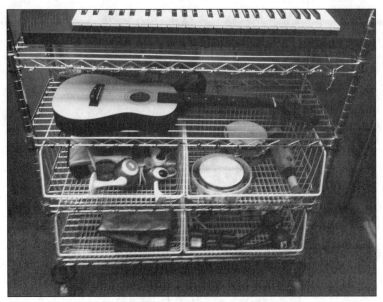
5.2: The completed cart ready to roll.

Samantha's work at Miami Children's Hospital didn't begin with offering to play music for the patients there. It began with working as a volunteer, bringing meals to the children's rooms. It was later that she recognized an opportunity to bring the music she loves to the patients she came to love. Having established a relationship with nurses and doctors working in the hospital, she was able to convince them to let the music of Travelin' Tunes nourish the spirits of the hospitalized children.

When Samantha was younger and dealing with her own illness, her great granddaddy introduced her to music. He played guitar and accordion, and at the age of eighty, began playing the piano. He used to invite Samantha to join him as he played and always let her play his instruments. The experience allowed her to temporarily forget her illness and relax and enjoy the experience of making music. He died when Samantha was in fourth grade; she inherited his keyboard. She began to practice and taught herself to play piano. Her parents encouraged her by paying for piano lessons and later by giving her great granddaddy's guitar and accordion. That's how Samantha came to love music and to recognize its power to soothe the spirits of the suffering.

Samantha now plays five instruments: piano, bass, cello, flute and guitar and she is, of course, proud of that accomplishment. Yet her real gratification comes from being with children. "I love working with kids. They are so smart and have so many interests. I find them quite inspiring."

Samantha's relationship with children in need has spread beyond Miami Children's Hospital. She recently took a trip to the Dominican Republic and brought instruments similar to the ones on her hospital cart, giving them to needy children. She plans to make a similar donation of instruments to an orphanage in another Latin American country. How does she get the money to buy these instruments? Well, that brings us to another dimension of Samantha's creativity and entrepreneurial disposition.

If you were to go to her website: http://pickapick.wix. com/pickapick#!portfolio you would find jewelry for sale— jewelry designed by Samantha using guitar picks. All of the proceeds from the sale of the jewelry go to support the work of Travelin' Tunes. Samantha is savvy enough to know that selling guitar pick jewelry, unique as that may be, will not raise sufficient funds for the kinds of humanitarian activities she wants to continue on behalf of kids, so she also came up with the idea of giving concerts.

Like any successful entrepreneur, Samantha knows it's critical to get others involved, using their available expertise to help bring a proposed activity to fruition. So when she came up with the idea of hosting a concert, she enlisted the aid of a friend, who helped her talk the local high school bands into participating. Her music teacher assisted in finding a venue for the concert and also helped coordinate the details.

Samantha acknowledges that a lot of people thought she was crazy when she announced she was going to organize a concert. She further admits there were times when she was trying to get that very first concert off the ground that she even thought they might be right. "At times I'd be very discouraged and I'd think, forget it; I don't care anymore. Then suddenly I'd realize, what am I saying? I love this. I need to be doing it." Three successful concerts later and Samantha was very happy that she had persevered.

Samantha has also received huge support and assistance from her immediate family. Her Mom is a teacher in the same school Samantha attends and she makes sure people in the school (and beyond) know when Samantha is planning to have a concert. She and Samantha's dad attend the concerts and help out with specific details. Dad also helps her with the financial and accounting side of things. Samantha's sister has helped her design the Pick-a-Pick website and, as Samantha says, continues to encourage her to be creative and imaginative. All of them are extremely proud of the inspiring humanitarian work that she is involved in.

Yet, beyond her family, Samantha receives the most encouragement from the children she plays for in Children's Hospital and their parents. The smile on their faces, their bursts of excitement, the tears in parents' eyes and the expressions of appreciation from everyone keep her energized and determined to continue and even expand her project.

Speaking of the children she works with, she explains, "I've seen so many children who have every right to be upset with the world and with people, but they are the happiest kids in the world." It is that kind of resiliency in the face of adversity that inspires Samantha and keeps her going. With all of the activities she is involved in and with her schoolwork, Samantha can be up as late as 3 AM. She says she has to prioritize, but that she always finds a way to do what she has to do.

On the subject of time, she'd like to remind adults that they still have ample time to transform the world, assuring a brighter future for all people. As for younger people, she is absolutely convinced that they are going to make a monumental difference in the world in the coming years. She certainly has. "My advice to young people," Samantha says, "is to just take a risk. Honestly, taking a risk is what gets a lot of people fired up to do what they believe in. If I set my mind to do something, it is going to happen. I don't know *how* it is going to happen, but I'll make it happen. Persistence, determination and passion are the three things you really need to do anything in life."

In 2011, Samantha was selected as one of Nestles' Very Best Youth Award Winners. She was honored for her work with the children at Miami Children's Hospital and was given a $1,000 grant for the charity of her choice. She donated the money to the Starlight Children's Foundation, a charity that is also dedicated to brightening the lives of seriously ill children and their families.

Honors and awards are not what Samantha is about, nor are they what give her the motivation to continue doing what

5.3: Samantha in 2013.

she is doing. "Honestly," she says, "for me to know that I've touched at least one person's life and that I've been a positive influence for them, that means the world to me." For young people like her, looking for inspirational words to motivate them to work to bring new hope to the world, Samantha cites the advice of an eleven-year-old boy suffering from a chronic illness whom she met at Miami Children's Hospital. "He had an ambiance and an eloquence about him that belied his years," she explains. His advice? "You need to pursue your dreams. Always believe in yourself. Work hard and just keep on going."

By the time she graduated from high school, the children's bedside music program at Miami Children's Hospital had been well established. When Samantha headed off to university, the original trio of Travelin' Tunes disbanded, yet a new generation of musicians continues the project. A junior now at Florida International University, Samantha occasionally visits the hospital where she used to volunteer, checking to insure that all of the instruments on the music cart are functioning and that the bedside music program is running smoothly.

Despite a demanding schedule at FIU where she is pursuing a degree in marketing and continuing to take courses toward a pre-med degree, Samantha's commitment to ensuring the well being of others has not diminished. She has become concerned about the plight of homeless in Coconut Grove, Florida and is determined to find ways to help them. And she will, since she has not forgotten the advice of that eleven-year-old boy, "Always believe in yourself. Work hard and keep on going."

That's great advice for one who wants to effect positive change. And if you are looking for a role model who epitomizes that philosophy, you have one in Samantha Fernandez.

6

the EggsChange Project

Love and kindness are never wasted.
They always make a difference.
They bless the one who receives them,
and they bless you, the giver.
~ Barbara De Angelis

When you go to a prestigious international school in a city like Shanghai and live in a protective bubble of a well-to-do community compound, it's difficult to be aware of, let alone empathize with, the plight of the rural poor. Yet even if you do become aware of the consequences of poverty in rural areas, what can you really do about it? In the rush and excitement of city life and the demands of school, the reality of rural poverty and those who suffer in it, is easily forgotten—out of sight, out of mind.

That's what makes the story of fifteen-year-old JinJin Xu so remarkable. Once she witnessed the reality of rural poverty, she didn't forget about it, and she didn't believe she was powerless to do anything about it. Instead, she hatched a micro-finance EggsChange Project that buys and then donates fifty chickens and the feed to sustain them, to individual rural farmers in GuangPi Village, JiangXi Province about 726 kilometers (451 miles) from Shanghai.

The selected farmers agree to raise the chickens according to free-range methods. They then sell the eggs produced by those chickens back to the EggsChange Project for a reasonable profit. EggsChange then sells these highly sought after eggs to customers in Shanghai, and with the money from those sales, the process continues and expands.

JinJin acknowledges that she and her classmates at Shanghai American School (SAS) live in an international community that is isolated from the local community, and in particular, the rural population. Travelling back and forth between their international school and their affluent living compounds, it's difficult for students to get a real sense of the disparity between their own standard of living and the locals' standard of living.

But JinJin didn't always live in that international community bubble unaware of what she describes as "the huge gap" between how the Shanghai international community lives and how the less fortunate in the villages beyond it live. Before her parents decided to send her to an international school, she attended local schools in Shanghai. Her Mom, who grew up in JiangXi, close to rural villages, used to take JinJin out to buy fresh produce to bring back to the family's home in Shanghai whenever they visited JiangXi. That's where JinJin saw the vast difference between her life and the lives of rural families. "I saw the state of poverty many lived in and I wanted to do something about it. I realized that while many farmers had the ambition to improve their lives, they lacked the opportunity to do so."

But what could she do? "The answer didn't come to my mind magically one night," she says. "I'd been thinking about it for a year and I didn't actually know how to go about solving that question." Then a confluence of small events that were part of her everyday life came together and resulted in the idea of the EggsChange Project. "I really like eating eggs. I'd sometimes eat three at breakfast until my Mom told me to stop because three were too many every day." When her Mom went back to visit her hometown, she brought back not only vegetables grown by rural farmers but eggs produced by their chickens as well. That's when JinJin found her answer.

Because people in Shanghai were becoming more aware of the dangers of chemicals and pesticides in their food products, they, like JinJin's mother, were looking for opportunities to buy healthy, "green" products directly from farmers. JinJin and her peers at Shanghai American School were already involved in a number of charitable fundraisers and community service projects; it was part of the school's culture, yet she wondered where the funds they raised actually went and how much good they accomplished in the long run. Donating money to a charitable cause was fine, but if its effect was merely temporary, how much more effective could a *project* be?

JinJin wanted to do more for rural farmers than merely give them a one-time handout; she wanted to give them something sustainable, something that would raise their standard of living and at the same time help them build something they could be proud of. Offering them an opportunity to generate a dependable weekly income for themselves would accomplish that goal. JinJin also had another vision for the farmers she planned to help, but we'll get to that later.

Recognizing that many of her schoolmates and their families loved eggs almost as much as she did, she saw an opportunity for helping rural farmers as well as her school peers. JinJin decided to propose a school club that would be different from any other club the school had previously created since it would in effect be a micro-finance, self-sustaining business.

When JinJin first presented her proposal to her principal, Ed Kidd, he was naturally skeptical. Here was a far-reaching proposal from an idealistic freshman whom he felt had no idea how difficult a project like this would be. He asked a lot of questions and pointed out certain things she had not considered. Their first meeting, he recalls, was basically a conversation about the germ of an idea she had, nothing more than that.

He recognized JinJin was really serious about her project when she returned to his office a few weeks later with a full-scale business plan and presentation. He was impressed. He agreed to help her find a faculty advisor who was equally convinced this project could succeed. That advisor turned out to be Mr. Koontz, JinJin's English teacher.

JinJin had never written a business proposal before so how she was able to design a comprehensive proposal that any businessman would be proud of is instructive and a testimony to her resourcefulness and perseverance. First, she went online and searched for *Proposal Writing for Dummies* and sat down and wrote one during a school break. Then she showed it to some English-speaking businessmen, friends of her father. Finally, she refined her proposal. "I looked at a few proposals that my Dad's friends had written for their companies and saw how they had structured them and how they used specific words."

In the EggsChange proposal, JinJin spelled out specific ways the project would benefit both rural farmers and SAS students. First, the project would provide farmers with a reliable source of weekly income and a direct connection with the world outside their village. And remember JinJin's other vision that we previously mentioned? The EggsChange Project would also be designed to give farmers guidance and support on how to start and run their own small business.

In her proposal, JinJin explained how the project would make SAS students aware not just of international problems but also of the rural poverty that was much closer to their homes. It would give them an opportunity to help alleviate that poverty, and because it was a micro-finance, non-profit project, it would give those who participated in it a glimpse into the management of various parts of running a small business: advertising and marketing, record keeping, and the logistics of sales and delivery.

Once she got the approval of the school principal to begin her EggsChange Project, JinJin's work had really just begun. Now she had to recruit other students. Together she and the other volunteers would have to organize major fundraising drives, as well as visit corporations in order to raise the money to buy chickens and their feed. Then the students would have to identify and interview the farmers who would most benefit from the project's donation and who would agree to raise the chickens using free-range principles.

The students would also have to arrange transportation for the chickens and feed from Shanghai to the farmers, and then transport the eggs from the farmers back to Shanghai where they would be sold. They would have to develop a system for keeping track of the money they received from the sale of eggs so that that money could go back to the farmers whose eggs they sold. Indeed, JinJin's business plan had made provisions for all of these demands.

6.1: Fifteen-year-old JinJin is speaking with one of the egg farmers, Tang Wen Ling in 2010 on her first trip to the GuangPi Village. Her friend and fellow student, Ihyun Park looks on.

In 2010, the EggsChange Project was initially staffed by a few of JinJin's friends. By 2013, there were fifty students involved and the project had donated chickens and feed to twenty farmers in GuangPi Village. The biggest challenge the project faced was selling the *volume* of eggs it received from its farmer partners, but JinJin and her club members came up with a number of innovative ways to deal with that challenge.

Along with establishing a system for selling their eggs to international families in community compounds surrounding their school, they also established a system whereby people could buy and donate eggs to retirement centers, homeless shelters, schools, hospitals or any charity of the donor's choice. Additionally, they partnered with members of the Roots and Shoots Club from their sister school in Pudong on the other side of Shanghai in order to expand both numbers of students involved and their potential for egg distribution. Another avenue that the project used to help with egg distribution was to reach out and entice managers in supermarkets, organic food stores and local markets to purchase their eggs.

Now in its fifth year of operation, the EggsChange Project has already registered many successes. It is providing farmers, mostly women, whose husbands and sons have had to leave for the cities to find employment, with a livable monthly salary of 1,400 RMB or $225. That may not seem like much of an income to many of us, but it has supported numerous rural families in improving their lives. One farmer was able to rebuild her house that had collapsed in a snowstorm, and she continues to provide financial support for her family— two daughters and a husband—even after her husband was injured in a factory accident and lost his job.

In addition to helping famers, JinJin's initiative has given poverty a real face for SAS students who have witnessed it first-hand. "When I first described to our club members how poor the rural farmers were," explains JinJin, "they were sort of used to poverty in the abstract sense because our school has so many fundraisers for poor people. But when we got to the village, they were shocked to see that just six hours away from where we live in fancy houses, there were people whose houses had collapsed. They were stunned to see the difference between the world we live in and this other world only a few hours away."

Despite its many successes, the EggsChange Project also had its share of frustrations and failures. The students' efforts to convince merchants to sell their free-range eggs was frustrating because, as JinJin says, they were teenagers and it was difficult to convince adult merchants to take them seriously. They experienced similar frustration when they initially attempted to open a bank account to wire money to the farmers. The bank was skeptical; these were merely students; how did they get so much money?

And then there was that 2012 experience at the Shanghai North American Auto Convention. The year before, when the EggsChange Project was in its infancy, JinJin and several of the project's officers had been warmly received at the convention and were given an opportunity to speak. They left having raised 4,000 RMB ($642). But on their second trip to the convention the students were not so warmly received, and after having spent most of the day and a good part of the evening outside the convention hall, they returned home having sold a mere fourteen of the ninety-six boxes of eggs that they had brought with them.

None of this discouraged JinJin, who is fondly referred to at her school as "The Egg Queen." She says that for every ten people that project members contact who reject their request for monetary donations, there is always someone who "gives us hope and is really excited about what we are doing and tries to help us with a donation or with advice." She and her schoolmates have learned from their mistakes and keep moving on. "On our second visit to the auto convention, we forgot to contact the organizers ahead of time," JinJin confessed. "We just showed up that day. It would have been better if we had given them a heads up that we were coming with boxes of eggs."

The EggsChange Project has been a great blessing for rural farmers who have benefitted from the love and kindness of JinJin and her classmates. Students from Shanghai

6.2: JinJin in Shanghai in 2013 just before leaving for the USA.

American School have also benefitted; they have come to know up close and personal the struggles of the rural poor in China—and that they have the power to relieve some of that poverty. Project members have also gained a great deal of business acumen.

But what about JinJin? Has this project been a blessing for her? JinJin speaks excitedly about how she has learned to supervise all the people involved, and how she and her peers have learned to be creative in solving problems that arise when managing a complex enterprise. She speaks with admiration and appreciation about the outstanding support she has received from her parents, her principal, her teachers and her peers. "I couldn't have done it without their support."

There is yet another learning experience that JinJin looks back upon with satisfaction—the experience of letting go, of passing the torch of leadership to her successors, Naomi Chan and Jennifer Gu. In 2013, JinJin graduated from SAS and traveled to Amherst College in Massachusetts where she is now in her sophomore year. She has stayed involved in the EggsChange Project in an advisory role, but it is her successors who have had to take on direct responsibility for ensuring that the work of the project continues—and they have! http://eggschange.weebly.com and eggs4change.org

The original twenty farmers are now financially stable. Their eggs are in high demand in rural villages nearby now that villagers have become aware of the EggsChange brand and the value of free-range eggs. As of this writing, the project has begun work with twelve new farmers and Naomi and Jennifer, about to graduate themselves and move on to college, have already trained and named their own successor, Julia Yoon.

It is when JinJin describes the heartwarming success stories of the farmers that her project has helped and how other students continue to step up and assume the leadership role she once held, that her sense of fulfillment really becomes palpable. "Now they know it can be done." That is the reward she considers her greatest blessing.

So when JinJin Xu advises those of us who want to help others to "dream big," we would do well to listen to her and remember all that she has accomplished by doing just that.

7

Hannah Has Heart

Americans are blessed with great plenty;
we are a generous people and we have a moral obligation
to assist those who are suffering
from poverty, disease, war and famine.
~ Adam Schiff, U.S. Representative, California

Hannah Moraes is now twenty years old. She attends California Lutheran College where she is majoring in Computer Science. She dreams of someday using her education to help others less fortunate, perhaps by distributing simple, programmable computers to children who can't afford them. Yet, back in 2006 when she was thirteen, Hannah gave a child a gift that was much more important than technology. This is her story.

Imagine for a moment what it must be like being born into a farming family in rural Vietnam with a congenital heart disorder. Your family has no insurance, in fact, no health care of any kind. You raise your own food and your only transportation is by foot. You live in a small wooden house with a metal roof and without indoor plumbing. Your water supply is outdoors. Family members' wants, and even many of their needs, can't be seriously considered.

There is no level of what would be called "comfort" by American standards. Your house is sixty square meters, roughly the size of a two-car garage. It is home to your extended

7.1: Hannah in 2014 on campus.

family of ten adults and children—about seven square yards per person of individual space. That's comparable to a large bathroom or a walk-in closet. But no person is entitled to any personal space; there just isn't enough room for that luxury. That is a life that thirteen-year-old Nguyen Thi Anh Thu doesn't have to imagine—she lives it.

Now consider that you are a middle school student who has relocated with your family to Vietnam; your father has been transferred there to work. You live in a comfortable international community composed mostly of Westerners and you are attending a well-financed international school. Vietnam is quite different from the state of Oregon where you once lived. Most American kids you know are from middle class families. Yet you soon learn that this is not the case for many Vietnamese families. In Ho Chi Minh City, you see children living in wretched poverty and it troubles you.

Looking from your window into a housing development under construction where Westerners like you will eventually live, you see migrant workers and their unkempt children walking around in rags and living in shanties on the construction grounds where new housing is being built for upper-middle class families.

That was Hannah Moraes' new reality when she moved to Vietnam. In time, she would become acutely aware of even greater difficulties in the lives of the Vietnamese families than the ones she could see from her window—and that new awareness would move her to action.

The East Meets West Foundation is an organization born of one woman's dream of helping to heal the wounds of war between the United States and Vietnam. The core of East Meets West's work is in the areas of learning, healing and health. So when one Vietnamese family sought the help of East Meets West for assistance with their child born with a serious congenital heart defect, Operation Healthy Heart was initiated.

Hannah learned of the efforts of Operation Healthy Heart when her mother borrowed a video of the East Meets West Foundation from a friend and brought it home to share with her family. After seeing the video, Hannah's first thoughts were of her father who had been born and raised in India. While his family was not poor, having food on the table had always been a priority. Some of his stories led Hannah to emotionally connect with people who lived in poverty and also helped her understand that she had been blessed to have been born into a family with "great plenty." She felt that she and others like her ought to be willing to help those less fortunate. She had not yet met Nguyen Thi Anh Thu, but their paths were soon destined to cross.

A few days after viewing the video, Hannah approached her mother and said that she wanted to do something to help Vietnamese kids who needed heart surgery, but whose families could not afford it. Her mother responded nonchalantly, "Okay, that sounds great, honey." Hannah realized that her mother was reacting to the fact that at times when she said she wanted to do something, she often didn't follow through with her idea. She was determined that this time would be different.

Hannah had to admit, though, that she was not sure how she would accomplish her goal, although a plan was beginning to take shape in her mind. During her summer break, she decided that one thing she could do was ask her church for financial help. She figured that there were about 2,000 people in her parish and if everyone gave just one dollar, then she might succeed. None of those churchgoers, she thought, would mind making such a small donation. And if they all made a donation, then she would have enough money to sponsor heart surgery for one child in Vietnam.

When Hannah presented her project to her family, her mother and father and her sister Hailey, enthusiastically supported it. Her parish priest also thought it was a great idea. The real challenge was getting up in front of that large audience, not once, but twice, since there were two masses each weekend. Hannah put together a speech, gathered up her courage and raised about $1,600 from an inspired audience.

Upon returning to Saigon South International School in September, Hannah connected with one of the directors of East Meets West, and that was how her path finally led to Nguyen Thi Anh Thu. After hearing what she had done during the summer, the Director of the Foundation made arrangements for Hannah to go and meet the young girl who had been waiting her entire life for critical heart surgery.

Nguyen Thi Anh Thu lived in Long An Province. Getting there required a two-hour car ride and a half-hour voyage on the Mekong River in a banana boat. Hannah remembers walking up the muddy bank of the Mekong to an unimpressive wooden structure with a tin roof that was home to Thu and her extended family. This was not a family, Hannah recognized, that could afford expensive medical care even if it meant the death of a child with a congenital heart defect.

Hannah noted that Thu was much smaller in stature and girth than she was, even though they were both thirteen years old. Because of her heart defect, Thu had always been frail. She was not only short, but also extremely thin. It shocked Hannah to realize that the fluttering she detected on Thu's chest through her shirt was her heart beating wildly. It was apparent to Hannah, even at her young age and without medical experience, that Thu's heart needed to beat rapidly to accomplish what most hearts easily do—supply oxygen and nutrition to her body.

Although Thu lived in a remote area of Vietnam, she spoke English remarkably well, making it easy for the two girls to communicate. So a comfortable bond was forged between them on that warm October day.

During Hannah's visit, Thu talked about how she tired easily. She told Hannah that she was often not able to attend school because she got so exhausted from the walk that she had to make each way. Even when she was able to go to school, she recognized that other children her age were able

7.2: Hannah with Nguyen Thi Anh Thu in 2006.

to run and play, while all she could do was sit and watch. She had lived her entire life knowing that life could be taken from her at any time, a fact which Hannah recognized as she watched the girl struggle for each breath.

Shortly after Hannah's visit with Thu and her family, Hannah's new friend was scheduled for open-heart surgery, a surgery made possible by Hannah's fundraising. When Thu was admitted to the hospital, Hannah went to visit her to give her a hug, hold her hand and wish her well. This was a critical moment for both girls. Thu faced major cardiac surgery, and Hannah faced the possibility that her new friend could be taken from her during the lengthy surgery that her efforts had made possible. For Thu, this surgery was a dream come true—an opportunity for which she had waited a lifetime. For her friend Hannah, it was a dream come true as well—the opportunity to give life to another.

Thu's family had waited a long time for an angel to walk into their lives and save their daughter. That angel, they believed, appeared in the form of Hannah Moraes. Although she did not have wings or a magic wand, Hannah had helped create the miracle that brought life back to their daughter.

Since that first surgery, Hannah has been instrumental in helping to raise funds for three additional surgeries for Vietnamese children. And so several miracles have happened because Hannah has heart.

When asked if this project has made a difference in *her* life, Hannah is quick to point out that it has made her feel like she has a special purpose. She says that she is not a hero, or an angel, as Nguyen Thi Anh Thu's family has portrayed her. While she certainly has heart, she says that she is just an average kid, not somebody special. Hannah sincerely believes that anybody can do what she did. "All they have to do is to get an idea and then make a plan and do it." Anyone can start with a really small idea, and that idea can grow into something quite substantial that makes a difference in the future of a person, family, community, country or even the world.

Hannah Moraes is a wonderful role model for everyone. Among those she has inspired is her sister Hailey, two years younger. Following in Hannah's footsteps, Hailey helped to organize a fundraiser called Laps for Lives at her elementary school in Ho Chi Minh City. During this event, some students run and others swim laps to raise money for a local orphanage. Among the spectators cheering her sister and her sister's schoolmates on is Hannah—Hannah, who has heart and who also recognizes "heart" in others.

8

Our Village, Our Family

I think one's feelings waste themselves in words;
they ought all to be distilled into actions, which bring results.
~ Florence Nightingale

Florence Nightingale answered a call to do good works through a cause, which was her most famous contribution during the Crimean War in 1853–1856. After she learned about the horrific conditions of the wounded who were moved from the battlefield to Turkey where the medical and sanitary conditions were nearly as abysmal as the battlefield, Florence traveled with a group of thirty-eight volunteer nurses that she had trained to help those who had been wounded.

In contemporary times, Nancy Brinker watched her sister Susan fight breast cancer and lose the battle. As she watched the life force ebb from someone she dearly loved, Nancy made a promise that she would do everything in her power to help find a cure for the cancer that was taking Susan's life. Thus, in 1982 she founded the Susan G. Komen Foundation in memory of her sister.

Both Florence and Nancy answered a call to help others in their own special way. You might wonder what a fifteen-year-old bicultural girl living in northern Thailand could have in common with Florence Nightingale and Nancy Brinker. Here is her story.

Kelly Perry remembers well that Christmas day in 2009 as she and her family awaited her mother's return from Bangkok so that they could open their Christmas presents. Yet when her mother arrived home, instead of experiencing the joy of opening presents, the family had to cope with the news that Kelly's mom had a suspicious lump in her breast that would require surgery to decide whether or not it was cancer. The good news for this family was that they had access to both excellent and affordable medical care that helped detect the dubious lump and then eliminate the fear of possible cancer. Indeed, Kelly's mother would eventually be fine.

Living in rural Thailand allows someone to become a member of the village where one lives; it doesn't matter that you live in a newer, Western style house with indoor plumbing and with what we might call the necessities of life, including a maid or two. You are a part of a village community; you live among the villagers and they think of you as part of their family. You feel about them the same way you feel about your own biological family. Although their houses are quite a bit smaller and they have few amenities, they are actually a part of your extended family. Each village also has a wizened elder who helps make some of the most important decisions regarding the village itself and those who live within it.

Kelly lives in a village called Tambon Chumpoo, filled with underprivileged people who make less than 150 baht per day ($5) either by farming or as construction workers in the city. By all stretches of the mind, Kelly Perry is indeed a Westerner. She also recognizes that she belongs not only to this village, but also to a greater society in which not everyone has equal access to quality medical care, or even the knowledge about what care is available.

8.1: A typical village dwelling in rural Thailand.

She has a Thai mother and an American father; she is bicultural and bilingual. Although she has traveled to the United States several times, Kelly has lived her entire life in Northern Thailand, where she is a student in Grade 10 at a private international school. Culturally, she is more Thai than American. While she moves easily amongst other cultures, Kelly knows and understands the people of Thailand, most especially the women within her village.

After the cancer scare that Kelly's mother and her family endured, Kelly found herself wondering why there was such disparity of medical care for the women who lived in Thailand. Thinking about this brought her to the conclusion that certain people by virtue of birth had access to high quality medical care, including the technology required for testing and diagnosing disease.

There were other women however, who didn't have access, nor did they have an understanding of what was available or why they would want to utilize that technology. Kelly's village was no exception; women who lived within this rural village had no knowledge of the advances in medical care and technology that now help save lives. They were blissfully unaware of the use of mammograms to support the early detection of breast cancer, which would allow women to be diagnosed and then treated so their lives could be saved.

Recognizing this fact, Kelly decided that she could help the women she knew and cared about in her village to understand what was available in medical care and why they needed to access it. What seemed to her like a simple enough task was daunting at best and totally disheartening at other times. What Kelly swiftly discovered was that those women were afraid of what they did not know and understand. Those that she knew and loved were not at all interested in having Kelly find ways to help them go to a hospital, take off their clothes and submit to the embarrassment and discomfort of a mammogram. They could never afford this service and they also didn't even want it.

Rural Thai women are extremely modest; likely they are some of the most modest of women in developing countries. If you have ever had a mammogram, you know that you must temporarily relinquish your modesty in order to complete the medical test that is so important in the detection of breast cancer. Indeed, this is a challenge for women of many cultures, Western cultures included. But, for rural Thai women, this is an obstacle beyond their wildest imagination. Most would rather die than to face the embarrassment required for this test.

So how, you might wonder, did a young girl of fifteen get the women of this rural village to agree to go to a hospital, take off their clothing from the waist up and have a screening mammogram?

Kelly quickly discovered that she would need an ally within the village. She made an appointment with the village elder, knowing that if she could convince this older woman, then she was on her way to getting support from the others. Unfortunately, Kelly's knowledge of mammograms and her ability to translate that knowledge into Thai was very challenging. So she met with doctors and hospital administrators to learn all that she could about this examination and how it was performed, and then she revisited the village elder armed with information to explain and discuss the options. For this second meeting, Kelly enlisted her mother's assistance in translating and explaining the procedure. In Thailand all must be done according to the appropriate protocol and that protocol dictated that this be an adult-to-adult conversation, with Kelly as a bystander.

Kelly worked diligently with her mother to explain her project and her hopes for a positive outcome. Then Kelly's mother discussed all the aspects they had talked about with the elder to help her understand both the medical process and the need. By enlisting the assistance of her mother, Kelly was able to show that this was a truly worthwhile undertaking.

Once Kelly had gained the respect of the village elder, she believed that the largest hurdle had been overcome. What she soon learned was that that was only the beginning. Kelly then began to work carefully on many fronts at the same time.

When she met with hospital administrators to let them know what she wanted to do, she swiftly found her next hurdle—cost. The fee for each mammogram would be 2,500 baht (approximately $80). After explaining her goal, Kelly was able to convince the director of Sri Pat Hospital in Chiang Mai to lower the cost of a mammogram by twenty percent to allow Kelly to include more women in her program at a lower cost.

To make mammograms available to all of the women in her village between the ages of 40 and 50 (the age group that she ascertained had the highest risk of developing or finding a lump or possible breast cancer), Kelly needed to raise over 94,000 baht ($3,000). She began the job of raising the required money. She received donations from supportive classmates who raised funds by selling paper hearts. Kelly sold items at a *sala*. Then she made presentations to potential donors at a pharmaceutical company. With these activities, Kelly managed to raise 75,515 baht ($2,500).

At this point, it was time to begin. A time, date and meeting place was set with scheduled appointments. Imagine the scene: twenty rural Thai women, along with the village leader climbing into the back of a pickup truck on their way to their first screening mammogram ever.

That day, Kelly had finally achieved her beginning goal, getting mammograms for twenty women in her village who might be at risk for breast cancer. Of those twenty, two were found to have lumps that needed further follow-up. Incredibly, once something suspicious was found as a result of the mammogram, the two women were then eligible to obtain treatment of an existing problem and only had to pay 30 baht (about $1). Now other women in the village were more likely to become aware of their breast health and what

8.2: *Tambon Chumpoo village women climbing into the truck for their first visit to the clinic in 2009.*

they could do for themselves. Kelly's next goal would be to identify additional women and expand the project to include an awareness program for all rural women in her area.

So, while it may be said that it takes an entire village to raise a child, it may also be said that it takes a child to raise awareness within that village, an awareness that may save the lives of the women most likely to develop breast cancer. As Kelly explains, "A little money and knowledge can go a long way toward helping women in rural Thailand to live longer and healthier lives without breast cancer. And if breast cancer does develop, then it can be found early enough to be treated and a life can be saved."

Kelly sees herself as providing a potential life-saving opportunity for these women who have no options for

8.3: Kelly in May 2014.

healthcare screenings. She says she is just another person who has done something to lessen what poverty has created, and what lack of knowledge has produced for people who weren't fortunate enough to have been born into the society that she was born into.

When we asked Kelly what she would say to other young people who would like to make a positive difference in the world, she told us: "Believe in yourself. You can't say it simpler than that. And once you believe in yourself, put your ideas on paper. It might be hard; you might think that it's difficult to help people, to make a difference. But once you get the ball rolling, it's not that hard. Act with your heart and let your passion support you in making a difference."

In June 2014, Kelly graduated from Chiang Mai International School. By that time, her goal of attaining breast cancer screenings for women in Tambon Chumpoo Village between the ages of 40 and 50 had been realized.

Kelly Perry is now attending Vanderbilt University in Nashville, Tennessee with plans to become a doctor. Although thousands of miles away from Thailand, she has not forgotten her commitment to providing healthcare opportunities for impoverished village women. Vanderbilt, she says, is passionate about having students perform community service. So she is planning to continue and expand her "Our Village, Our Family" project as an undergraduate student.

9

Disposing of Poverty

Is education to be a "passport to privilege,"
or is it something that people take upon themselves
almost like a monastic vow, a sacred obligation to serve people?
~ E. F. Schumacher

"Ask people who their heroes are and you might get answers like Oprah Winfrey, David Beckham or Bill Gates. My hero is a man who made his living scavenging through trash." If you think this is an unusual way to introduce yourself to the faculty of the university you hope to attend, it is. But that is the way that Cecilia Martinez Miranda introduced herself to the faculty at Macalester College in her admission essay.

The choice of a Filipino trash picker as a hero is unusual, but what makes the choice even more exceptional is that the young woman who has chosen him comes from a Filipino family of privilege. The man Cecilia is referring to is Manuel Manarang. He grew up in the Smokey Mountain dumpsite of Tondo, Manila and scavenged the two million ton site for twenty years. He got lucky and eventually managed to escape from Smokey Mountain, get an education and a job elsewhere. But he and his wife Victoria eventually made a decision to return to the Philippines and devote themselves to improving the lives of the poor in Smokey Mountain where they had grown up.

Manarang would ultimately become a co-founder of WE International Philippines, an offshoot of WE International, an organization devoted to reducing poverty in Third World countries by promoting economic development through education, micro-lending, and encouraging sustainable business growth. One of his co-founders at WE International Philippines is eighteen-year-old Cecilia Martinez Miranda.

The admissions director chose to accept Cecilia's application to attend Macalester College in St. Paul, Minnesota. She carries a double major in Education and International Studies. Her minor is in Political Science, with a concentration in International Development. That's a hefty academic load, but Cecilia has a mission in life. She intends to help improve the lives of the less fortunate. The subjects she is studying, she knows, will help her fulfill that mission.

At Macalester, in addition to attending class, Cecilia is deeply involved in humanitarian work. She and a fellow student, Michael Manansala recently received a $10,000 grant from the Davis Project for Peace to help students and their teachers at a Container School in Tondo install a vertical vegetable and herb garden, as well as a rainwater collection system, making it possible for them to grow food to use in the school's cafeteria. (The Container School has been constructed from recycled shipping containers and provides free education for 1,000 students from Smokey Mountain.)

Cecilia was born into a well-to-do family; her father worked for the World Bank and her mother owned her own business. Her parents could afford to send her to the prestigious Brent International School in Manila as she was growing up. Yet Cecilia didn't always appreciate the disparity between the life she led and the lives of children less fortunate. She recalls that as she was driven to school each day, whenever the car slowed down or came to a stop, underprivileged children would approach, knock on the windows and try to sell her flowers, cheap jewelry or other small trinkets. Unlike her parents, the parents of these children could not afford to send them to school. At the time, though, that did not make much of an impression on her.

It wasn't until she was fourteen and traveled to Sweden with her soccer team that the stark contrast between her situation and that of the children who were knocking on their car window hit home. Walking the streets of Gottenberg, she suddenly realized that here, unlike in the Philippines, there were no people sleeping in boxes on the sidewalks, and there were no children trying to sell flowers. "It was the first time that I realized that those situations we had in the Philippines weren't inevitable." Other "ah-ha" moments were soon to follow.

On a school-sponsored volunteering trip with Gawad Kalinga (a group similar to Habitat for Humanity), she asked one of the young residents what he wanted to be when he grew up. He told her that he wanted to be a doctor. "But," he added, "I'm probably going to be a mechanic because my parents don't have the money to send me to school." It was then that Cecilia says she realized that what kids decide to do in life often has more to do with the opportunities open to them than with their innate talent and intelligence. She remembers thinking that given the right circumstances this kid could become President of the Philippines.

It is this recognition that opportunity, as much as talent and intelligence, controls what a person can achieve in life that drives Cecilia's humanitarian efforts. She is determined to open doors of opportunity for those less fortunate than she is. "We don't ask for the situation that we are born into," she explains. "But it doesn't matter where we begin; it's more about where we go from *there* that matters." She understands that for certain people, getting from where they were born to where they want to go is much more of a challenge than for others. She recalls the first time she visited the Smokey Mountain dumpsite with Manuel Manarang. "I distinctly remember the noise my boots made as we trudged through the sludge, and the overwhelming sticky sour stench that seemed to invade my every pore."

Education is key to opening doors of opportunity for everyone, for those who are as fortunate as she and for those who are far less fortunate, like the children of Smokey Mountain. Cecilia plans to use her own education as a means to fight for quality educational opportunities for disadvantaged Filipinos. Manuel is her inspiration, her symbol of hope. Just as education provided him with an opportunity to escape from scavenging the dumpsite for a living, she knows that it is an avenue of freedom for others as well. And just as his education inspired him to return to Smokey Mountain to help others escape from poverty, she knows that the right kind of education can inspire others like her to want to follow in Manuel's footsteps.

Yet, what kind of education is the right kind of education? For Cecilia it is an education that makes a person more than simply "smart." It is an education that makes us aware of our shared humanity, that we are all people of worth, some of us more fortunate than others.

She reflects that it is also useful to learn that being more fortunate doesn't necessarily make us better than others,

9.1: Cecilia and Kuya Manuel Manarang in 2009 with children living at the Smokey Mountain dumpsite in Tondo, Manila.

only luckier. Those who are privileged, she believes, should see their good fortune as an opportunity and a mandate to help others. "I have been given opportunities my whole life and if I was given a chance, it shouldn't be hard to extend opportunities to others," she says. Thinking back to her experience with Gawad Kalinga and the young man she met who wanted to be a doctor but believed he would never get the opportunity, keeps Cecilia focused on her goal of looking at education and educational systems as a way to channel possibilities for all youngsters to achieve their dreams.

Cecilia is a visionary systems thinker. She won the Ann Bolger Vision Award at Macalester, honoring a student leader who initiates positive organizational change or creative endeavors to contribute to the educational experience of students in a thoughtful, collaborative, and informed fashion. She has brought Macalester students with her to work in the Philippines, but her real focus is on social entrepreneurship, identifying challenging social problems, designing long-term sustainable solutions for them, and enlisting others to become part of those solutions.

Like many of our other heroes, Cecilia's involvement in humanitarian work began small. While in high school, she was involved in student government, and in her own words was engaged in "a lot of random things." One activity brought her to a public hospital where she met janitors, most of whom were women, working in the hospital to pay off their children's medical bills. While this was a formative experience for Cecilia, the defining moment was meeting with the young boy who wanted to be a doctor. It was then that she decided she wanted to go into education, and not only be in it, but also examine how education creates channels of opportunity for some, while failing to create them for so many others. Her goal is to reverse that failure.

Cecilia and her colleagues at WE International feel that reversing that failure will require a two-pronged approach: top-down and bottom-up. And so, even as they work with children from the slums, they also work with students in private schools and in colleges, encouraging them to find solutions for poverty and inequality. She took this initiative of challenging the fortunate to find ways to help the unfortunate to Macalester College, where she continued searching for opportunities to engage students on campus.

Among the many strong personal qualities that Cecilia possesses is a capacity for deep reflection and honesty. She is constantly looking for sustainable solutions to the innumerable problems she sees around her, but she acknowledges she hasn't found many satisfactory solutions yet. She isn't hesitant about saying, "I haven't figured that out yet"; or "We're going to have to work out the best way to do that." Uncertainty, however, doesn't keep Cecilia from persisting in looking for answers or from continuing to work with the partial solutions she and her WE colleagues have discovered.

Cecilia continues to move forward on the assumption that one of the best ways to change the situation at Smokey Mountain is to give young people there opportunities to get out of that environment and see the world elsewhere. She understands the criticism of the leader of another non-governmental organization (NGO) who told her that having a broader vision isn't the best way; that the best way is to help people to find hope within their Smokey Mountain environment. "But," she counters, "when you talk to many of the children we work with in Smokey Mountain who have never been exposed to anything outside of that environment and ask them what they want to be when they grow up, they tell you they want to be a garbage truck driver."

So Cecilia encourages her colleagues to find ways to expose Smokey Mountain youth to the world beyond by getting them out of that setting and bringing people from the outside world into that environment to expose both groups to a different world view. Once they have escaped Smokey Mountain and have lived life elsewhere, Cecilia hopes these young people will return home and improve the conditions there, as Manuel Manarang and his wife have, and as she plans to do once she has completed college. She wants to see young Filipino entrepreneurs return to the Philippines and work with communities, like the one in Smokey Mountain, to create sustainable enterprises that will change conditions for those who live there.

She explains that the more young people look at the systems we, as a society, have put in place, the more they realize that these systems are not the systems we actually need. The current systems leave too many people out. We have to find ways to replace these failing systems with new, more dynamic and inclusive ones. Young people must be key players in this renewal effort because they haven't been socialized to see *only* what they have been taught. They can see what they and their society might be able to achieve. They have not yet learned to put themselves in boxes and limit their potential.

Cecilia encourages young people to get involved, be creative, trust their instincts and believe that they can make the world a better place for everyone. As for adults, she explains that the best thing that they can do for young people is to have faith in their possibilities and support their desire and efforts to be the best that they can be for the world.

While her studies kept her away from the Philippines for much of her time at Macalester College, Cecilia continued to work for WE International. Her Davis Project for Peace was one of her initiatives on behalf of the young people at Smokey Mountain. Even while she was away at college, she continued to find ways to engage in humanitarian projects and build her social entrepreneurship skills. She spent one summer working with the Ashoka Youth Venture, a global community of young change makers. She also worked with an organization called Old Arizona in the Twin Cities, where she helped set up a teen-run flower shop, a social

9.2: Cecilia shortly after her graduation.

entrepreneurship project for inner city girls aged thirteen to sixteen.

There are, of course, those who worry that a young humanitarian like Cecilia might focus so singularly on the needs of those less fortunate that she will neglect her own needs. While Cecilia understands those concerns, she knows that her education, plus the practical experience she is gaining working for NGOs (writing grants, establishing micro-finance projects, planning projects for sustainability, meeting people from different cultures and diverse socio-economic tiers, as well as working to engage other people in humanitarian work) will equip her with the knowledge and skill set that she will need in the future.

In early 2013, Cecilia Martinez Miranda graduated from Macalester College. True to her commitment to return to the Philippines to help find sustainable solutions to improve the lives of the disenfranchised there, Cecilia assumed the role of Executive Director of WE International Philippines. In 2014, WE International was temporarily disbanded due to issues affecting the larger Smokey Mountain community. The dumpsite where they were working was shut down, and its residents relocated outside of Metro Manila.

The knowledge that this change hasn't improved the fortunes of most of those who scavenged at the site reminds the group that there is still much work to be done. Though difficult, this change has allowed the WE team to reflect and take time to focus on each of the team members' own projects. They hope that they will one day be able to regroup and strategically continue WE International's mission and vision.

Even as she continues to work with WE International Philippines to establish a new direction for the organization, Cecilia has extended her reach in another direction. She is currently working with her family on a project to develop a property in Merida, Leyte. When finished, that project will hopefully create new business opportunities and new jobs for men and women there. She has, she says, found that there are many ways to make a positive difference in the world.

10

Helping Angels with Broken Wings Fly

I have always held firmly to the thought
that each one of us can do a little
to bring some portion of misery to an end.
~ Albert Schweitzer

Disabled is defined as unable to perform, restricted, powerless. Unfortunately, the word itself stigmatizes those labeled with it. It focuses on the wrong thing, what people *can't* do rather than what they *can* do. In essence, it separates them from the rest of us, the "abled," and causes many of us to shy away from, and, in some cases, avoid contact with those who are handicapped. But not Jiayi (Daniel) Huang; he embraces disabled people—whole groups of them. Daniel is currently a sophomore at Brandeis University in Waltham, Massachusetts, but his efforts on behalf of disabled individuals began when he was a high school junior at Beijing City International School.

Daniel is a serious young man whose interests, by his own admission, are different from most kids his age. He finds pop music loud and distracting; he likes classical music instead. He prefers history and photography to basketball and other sports. And he is committed to helping people less fortunate than he is. That commitment led Daniel, while still in high school, to create Help Angels With Broken Wings Fly, an organization dedicated to supporting disabled people. Simultaneously, he strives to raise "abled" peoples' awareness of the talents, abilities, enduring spirit and perseverance of those with emotional or physical infirmities.

The title of his organization is testimony to how Daniel views the disabled people he works with. They are angels— angels whose broken wings prevent them from chasing their dreams like others do. "What we are trying to do," he explains, "is to give handicapped people new wings."

Daniel admits that he didn't always have an understanding of, or an appreciation for, disabled individuals and what they could accomplish. "I thought those who were disabled couldn't do anything—that since they were physically challenged, they stayed at home." His ignorance, however, was transformed to insight and admiration as a result of a project involving several students from Peking University.

Daniel comes from a family of doctors. His mother is a cardiologist. His grandmother was a neurologist and his father was an orthopedic doctor before deciding to go into business. His mother is also a professor who works at the Medical Center of Peking University. She assigned her students a project in which they were to investigate the health conditions in the local community; she also introduced her son to her students and got him involved in the project as well. That project is what eventually stirred Daniel's interest in people with disabilities and resulted in his commitment to helping them, as well as encouraging others to do likewise.

During his work with the university students, Daniel discovered that there were about 300 rehabilitation centers located throughout China run by the Federation of Disabled People in Beijing. He knew that disabled individuals lived in and were cared for in these centers. But he wondered what they did with their time while living there. What was it like spending all your time not doing anything productive?

Daniel spoke to one of his friends who had a connection with a director in the Federation of Disabled People and arranged for them to meet. After the meeting, the director invited them both to visit the Jingshan Community Rehabilitation Center. What Daniel witnessed during that visit resulted in the formation of the Help Angels With Broken Wings Fly (FLY) Project.

Contrary to what he had imagined, Daniel learned during his visit that the disabled "angels" in the Center were not sitting around doing nothing. In addition to learning life skills, they were making handicrafts in the center's workshop that were to be sold. He learned too, that making these handicrafts allowed the residents to experience a sense of pride and self-worth, and that they could be productive and contribute something to society. But there was also a problem.

The crafts the residents were making were not selling well, and while the funds the Center received from the government were enough to maintain it, if the handicrafts didn't sell, the Center would not have money to buy the raw materials that would allow the residents to continue to produce them.

When that happened, the director told them, the handicapped residents would no longer feel they were contributing to society and their sense of self-worth would deteriorate.

The problem with the lack of sales, Daniel found out, was a consequence of the fact that the Center's director didn't have connections with the business community, and there was no one to help market the handicrafts. Daniel saw his opportunity. "I decided to be the person to market those products for them."

10.1: Sample handicraft product of the residents of the Jingshan Community Rehabilitation Center.

Daniel persuaded a couple of friends to join him in the task he had chosen to undertake. Of course it's one thing to decide to do something and quite another to figure out how to do it effectively. "It was really hard to start because we had no experience at all in marketing." So he and his friends embarked on what Daniel calls his Word of Mouth Strategy. They let other friends know about their proposed project and asked them to help spread the word to other people in the community.

It may not sound like much of a marketing strategy, but it worked. Soon more and more people became aware of their project for the disabled residents of the Jingshan Rehabilitation Center. People began to call and order the handicrafts. The three young marketers also made a video and designed posters. They visited the market areas in Beijing and established a connection with several shop owners who agreed to sell the Center's handicrafts. As a result, they made several hundred RMB (Chinese yuan) in profit for the Center.

But there were plenty of rejections too, since more shop owners turned them down than accepted their proposition. Daniel was disappointed but not discouraged. He recognized that his project was not just about raising money. A few hundred or even a few thousand RMB would do little toward helping handicapped workers feel like self-sufficient contributing members of society. Much more needed to be done, but what, and how?

Then something serendipitous happened. When he returned to school at Beijing City International School (BCIS) after summer break, Daniel's high school principal, Craig Rodgers, asked him what he had done during his summer vacation. Daniel told him and Rodgers was impressed. "Daniel is not a 'tell the world' kind of young man," Rodgers says. "It was almost by accident that I discovered what he was doing and his vision for what he hoped to achieve at the Jingshan Community Rehabilitation Center." Rodgers was so impressed that he asked Daniel to present his project to BCIS students at a high school/middle school assembly.

A week after Daniel's school assembly presentation, the BCIS marketing department invited him to set up a booth and sell the Center's crafts at the school's Christmas Bazaar and also the Temple Fair that would be part of the school's celebration of the Chinese New Year in January. He was very excited and saw these two venues as a perfect opportunity to expand his project. Still, success seldom comes without persistence, as Daniel was to learn over and over again. Two problems soon arose that put the prospect of selling the crafts at the Christmas Bazaar in jeopardy.

The first was that the marketing department at the school informed Daniel a few weeks later that they were having trouble finding space for him at the bazaar and suggested he put off selling the crafts until the Temple Fair in January. Daniel was concerned that the delay would result in a shortage of money with which to buy the necessary raw materials to keep the Community's workshops going.

He sent a number of emails to his school's marketing department expressing his concern about their decision and asked to meet with them. After several face-to-face talks with the director, he was given one of the best locations for his booth at the bazaar. But then another major problem arose.

The timing of the bazaar coincided with a difficult time for Daniel's two local school partners. They were near the end of their middle school years and were preparing to move on to high school; they didn't feel they had time to help with the Christmas Bazaar. So, Daniel was on his own. He admits that this was a time when he felt a lot of pressure and became a bit discouraged. But instead of letting the stress and disappointment deter him, he just got more creative.

He recruited a few new volunteers to help him organize and sell, first for the bazaar and then the Temple Fair, and also for future opportunities. He posted a video on Renren, a Chinese Social Network similar to Facebook. As a result, the Help Angels With Broken Wings Fly Project raised over 12,000 RMB (approximately $1,850) for the Center. Daniel says that the funds helped boost the confidence of the disabled people in the Jingshan Community by showing them that they *were* valued by their society.

Daniel's success in fundraising activities didn't represent the end of his quest to help handicapped people find meaning

10.2: Daniel at the Helping Angels Fly booth in January 2012, at the Beijing City International School [BCIS] Temple Fair.

and purpose in their lives. It was, he explains, only the starting point. He developed several short-term six-month goals for FLY. He continued recruiting volunteers from BCIS to interact and speak with the members of the Jingshan Community. He explained, "We have an opportunity to help these disabled people realize they are not alone and do not need to be marginalized by the greater Beijing community."

He also investigated the possibility of opening an online store on Taobao (the Chinese version of eBay) so that the Jingshan Center's handicrafts would be more accessible to all Chinese people. That option has yet to be realized because, as Daniel discovered, the FLY Project must apply for a license to sell online. Daniel did, however, build a strong connection between the Jingshan Center and Pfizer Corporation, which has resulted in Pfizer regularly purchasing handicrafts from the Center to give to customers and business partners.

Daniel was also successful in convincing the Peking University Health Science Center (PUHSC) to provide free monthly services, including counseling services, to members of the Jingshan Community. Before he left for university, Daniel learned that PUHSC had offered an option for its medical students to conduct their graduation projects at the Jingshan Community Center.

The plight of the disabled in China at the present time is most often a dismal one. In rural areas, physically handicapped babies are sometimes just abandoned. In the cities, strong regulations prohibit discarding disabled infants, but then these children simply grow up to become beggars or thieves. Those physically handicapped children who end up in rehabilitation centers, although rejected by the general population, are among the more fortunate ones. "In China," says Daniel, "people don't like disabled people; they are just excluded from society."

Daniel is determined to change that long-held view. Perhaps his most ambitious ongoing goal is to raise the awareness of the Chinese people about the strengths, as well as the needs, of emotionally and physically disabled people, and to generate more understanding of, and compassion for them. He is convinced that everyone has at least a bit of compassion, and he wants to give each person an opportunity to put it to good use on behalf of those angels with broken wings. "Disabled people need us. We need to help them. We can't just leave them alone."

Before graduating from Beijing City International School, Daniel made two additional decisions to ensure that the organization he founded will continue to help Chinese angels with broken wings fly in his absence. In June, after learning that students from fifteen universities in the United States, including Yale, Harvard, Brandeis, John Hopkins and UT Austin annually come to China to study Mandarin as part of a Continuing Education and Training Program (CET), Daniel received permission from the CET staff to conduct a US-Sino Student Disability Forum. The forum brought students from those fifteen universities together with ten students from the Peking University Health Science Center (PUHSC) to discuss the care that the disabled receive in both countries. Daniel made a presentation and moderated the forum, thus creating a bond between the US universities and PUHSC, ensuring that China's healthcare providers learned about new practices they could adopt for their care of the disabled.

Additionally, Daniel made a choice that he acknowledges was difficult for him. Rather than try to direct the FLY Project from a distance, he relinquished his leadership of the program to a group of fifteen very committed BCIS high school students. This ongoing project, which he checks on periodically, is continuing with the momentum he established. And if you think that Daniel is finished helping angels with broken wings fly, you are wrong. Daniel is currently a student at Brandeis University in Waltham, Massachusetts and he is working on plans to launch a FLY Project in the United States.

Like all the young people in this book, Daniel Huang downplays his accomplishments. While acknowledging that his project has had a positive impact on the handicapped people he's worked with, he doesn't feel that what he is doing is anything spectacular. He says that the difficulties he occasionally faces in his own life cannot be counted as difficulties when compared to the challenges his angels in the rehabilitation centers face.

10.3: Daniel's speech at the 2014 International Conference Forum in Beijing.

His advice to other young people who want to help others is, "Everyone can make a difference, everyone can do something positive for society. It's not as difficult as you may think. Have courage and just try to do it. The important thing is to keep on going—keep on doing it—your whole life."

11

the Social Responsibility Foundation

"I must do something"
always solves more problems than
"Something must be done."
~ Author Unknown

Robert Li is now a sixteen-year-old student. Born in Canada, he has lived in China for the past twelve years attending Shanghai American School. He is Chinese, and like many young people in China today, Robert has no siblings—a result of the one child policy instituted by the government in September 1980. What Robert does have is an abundance of compassion. "My whole life I have always enjoyed helping people around me, whether it be a stranger, my friends, my teachers or my family," he explains.

That commitment to helping people eventually led Robert, while still in middle school, to establish the Social Responsibility Foundation (SRF). SRF is a non-profit organization whose mission is to promote the development of youth social responsibility, to strengthen young people's sense of civic engagement, and to extensively publicize the idea of alleviating poverty by giving micro-credit loans to underprivileged people in rural China.

Now that may sound like an ambitious vision for a young man who was only twelve at the time, but there is something else about Robert. In addition to his compassion, his conviction is that young people have an obligation to help make the lives of the less fortunate better. "I'd like to see more young people do good things, as well as keep in mind that there are others in this world who are not financially well off and require our help and support."

So how does a twelve year old begin to create an organization that now, five years into its establishment, has over three hundred members, not just in China but in a number of other countries as well? That's Robert's story.

Up until the age of twelve, Robert had participated in programs that raised money and donated to disadvantaged, struggling people. But these were one-time donations, and despite his age, Robert knew that while that money provided temporary relief, these one-time donations seldom substantially changed the lives of the people who received them. He wanted to do something that would have a more lasting effect. He found a way quite by accident.

Most people have heard of Asian societies' tradition of the red packet (or red envelope). In China during the Lunar New Year holiday, it is traditional for older people to give younger relatives a gift of money in a red packet. The red packet is supposed to bring good luck to those who receive it. As it turned out, it did bring Robert good luck. Because of the red packet, he discovered the micro-finance organization that would lead him to establish his own.

"During Chinese New Year of 2009, I received a yearly sum of red packet money. That year, I was seeking a better way to invest my money, as I rarely needed to spend any of the red packet money I received," Robert recalls. The bank interest rates were low at that time and Robert searched the Internet to find a place where he would get a better interest rate. By chance he came upon Yinongdai. Although this wasn't exactly what he was looking for when he began searching for a higher rate for his red packet money, it turned out to be a great find in another way.

Yinongdai is a P2P (Peer to Peer), online, micro-finance lending platform that allows people to connect with, and lend to, the poor (primarily women farmers) in rural China. Lenders go online, see a picture of the potential borrower, read a brief biography and review her needs and plans. Individual lenders can then donate as little as 100 RMB (about $16), or as much as they want.

Because the money is a loan rather than a donation, the borrower must agree to pay back that loan with a minimal interest rate in quarterly installments. Once the loan is paid back, as it is almost 100% of the time, the lender can get his money back with a small 2% earning, or leave it in his account and lend it to another borrower.

Here was a way, Robert recognized, to ensure that his compassion would have a much more lasting effect. Here was a way to help alleviate poverty in rural areas by giving people loans that helped them establish their own self-sustaining businesses. As the old proverb counsels, "Give a man a fish and you feed him for a day; teach a man to fish and you feed him for a lifetime."

Robert turned to his father, a venture capitalist whose firm Tsing-Capital invests in green technology, to find out more about micro-financing. Robert's dad knew about CreditEase, the micro-finance company that launched Yinongdai in 2009. He explained to his son the ideas behind micro-credit and the

11.1: School photo taken in early 2012,
Robert's junior year in high school.

fact that the 2006 Nobel Peace Prize winner, Dr. Mohammad Yunus, had practiced this concept for more than thirty years.

Robert read about Dr. Yunus and spent time doing additional research on the goals and the process of micro-financing until he felt ready. With a strong grasp of the theoretical underpinnings, he approached a couple of his closest friends and announced his intention to set up a nonprofit, philanthropic organization. He invited them to join him. He told them that he believed that young people had a responsibility to make the world better. "In a few decades the world is going to be ours, and if none of us are willing to do something positive for this world, who will?" He told his friends that the best way for them to make a difference was through micro-finance activities dedicated to improving the lot of the rural poor. They agreed. Thus was born the Social Responsibility Foundation (SRF).

It was a small beginning, but SRF grew and spread using the P2P approach that Yinongdai supported. He and his friends approached peers at their own school first, and then students at other international schools in China and beyond. Most youths in Asia get red packet money. Robert and his friends encouraged others to invest that money in micro-financing programs like Yinongdai instead of spending it on themselves.

Still, Robert realized, it's one thing to see a picture of a rural farmer on the Internet and read about her needs, and quite another to see first-hand the plight of the rural poor. Robert took a field trip sponsored by Yinongdai to the county of Laishui to see what poverty was really like and to observe how micro-finance loans can help relieve it. "Until you actually go there, you don't understand what the life of a poor farmer looks like or how this process can help them."

Two memories from his trips to rural villages are etched in Robert's mind. They will always be a reminder to him of the difference someone can make in another person's life. The first is of a struggling young woman who was given a micro-finance loan and used it to open a barbershop in her village. She was doing quite well as a result. The other memory is of a farmer and his wife who were living in a rudimentary shack only 100 kilometers (60 miles) from Beijing. It was freezing cold and the farmer and his spouse were sleeping on the floor of this roughly built dwelling. Yet they had somehow managed to send their four children to university, wanting a better life for them. He realized how a micro-finance loan might improve their lives.

Those two pictures of the challenges of life in rural villages have made Robert determined to continue to expand the work of his Social Responsibility Foundation. In addition to the expansion of its membership, the SRF now helps Yinongdai organize field trips to rural villages so that young donors can interact with the villagers, see the real face of poverty, and observe for themselves how their donations can change that face from one of anxiety and hopelessness to one of hope and joy.

While they are on these field trips, the young people in SRF engage in a number of other humanitarian activities. They bring books and other school supplies to the villages. They have also started teaching both children and adults basic health care, such as how to properly brush one's teeth and how to administer first aid. Recently SRF raised funds to purchase solar lamps for classrooms that didn't have electricity.

Robert continues to extend the reach of SRF. In the five years since he founded it, membership has grown to 453 young people. SRF now has eight chapter affiliates, including ones in Switzerland, Australia, New Zealand, and the United States; it has given 365,600 RMB ($58,735) in loans to 2,868 rural families.

In March 2013, SRF evolved from being a simple non-profit into a social enterprise business. It continues to provide micro-credit loans to women in rural areas and to provide the children of these women with increased educational opportunities. It remains committed to teaching English and educating rural families about daily healthcare, while offering first aid classes in village schools. Now it also has begun to help farmers organize rural production cooperatives and study groups, assisting them in establishing channels of

11.2: Robert presenting the Intel Social Innovation Week TED talk when he was sixteen.

distribution (both online and off-line) for their agricultural products. SRF is also beginning to promote health and agricultural insurance in rural communities. You can find his website at www.SRFChina.org.

In June 2013, Robert and five other students formed a team to compete in a SAGE tournament. SAGE (Students for the Advancement of Global Entrepreneurship) is an international non-profit that offers teens an opportunity to showcase their social enterprise businesses and business plans in both national and worldwide competitions. In these tournaments, teams are judged by a panel of influential members of the business, social and educational communities. SAGE founder Dr. Curtis DeBerg established these tournaments to counter the notion often held by hard-nosed business people that it is "unrealistic and overly idealistic" to believe that teenagers can make the world a better place.

Robert and his team didn't win the SAGE tournament, yet they were declared first runner-up. But winning wasn't their ultimate goal anyway—learning was. "It was a great learning opportunity," Robert explains. "The SAGE program provides a series of training sessions on setting up a social business, while also offering free consulting services from industry specialists." For Robert, participation in the SAGE competition was merely a means to an end. The end? Continuing efforts to help make the world a better place for the less fortunate.

Robert tells us, "I have visited those whom I have personally assisted in rural Laishui, Dingxi, Yanchi and Ningxia and witnessed their impressive accomplishments. When I saw the smiles on the faces of rural Chinese villagers, I knew that I, a mere teenager, was able to make a difference in this world. No effort in this direction is too small, and united, we adolescents will be able to shout loudly with our actions. The responsibility to better this world beyond the self is ours."

In June 2014, Robert Li graduated from Shanghai American School. He is currently a freshman in the Wharton School of Business at the University of Pennsylvania. The Wharton School, as Robert points out, offers great opportunities for micro-finance studies and has a large on-campus college micro-finance club. That club sponsors an annual micro-finance conference and Robert plans to support SRF by "leveraging the power of the Penn student body and alumni network to further the work of SRF in helping farmers in China and other developing countries." Congratulations, Robert!

12

An Invitation to Relieve Poverty

We all participate in weaving the social fabric;
we should therefore all participate in patching the fabric
when it develops holes.
~ Anne C. Weisberg

When she speaks about social issues and global problems, you can't miss the earnestness in her voice. Priscilla Acuna Mena, age seventeen, is a dedicated humanitarian who appeals to young people to become actively involved in tackling the global challenges of our time. "We must do something as soon as possible; it's incredibly urgent. Take the 30,000 children who die from poverty-related causes every day. Every few seconds costs lives. We can't simply wait for someone else to solve the social issues of our time. We may be young, but we're not powerless."

This sense of urgency comes from Priscilla's personal encounters with the face of poverty. She saw it first in the expressions of children in the Philippines and later in the faces of young people in Jakarta, Indonesia. She feels strongly that all people, but especially people her age, have a responsibility to do something to relieve the injustice that is all round them, but that too often remains hidden from plain sight. "Young people," she says, "can't evade their own personal responsibility by thinking, 'Well yes, we have a problem, but let someone else, let the *adults* take care of it.'"

Priscilla's own commitment to helping those less fortunate is obvious in the things she says, but even more so in the things she does. She explains that she first intended to devote her life to helping others after she spent a summer volunteering with a local non-governmental organization (NGO), *Yayasan Usaha Mulia* (YUM) in Indonesia.

But Priscilla is more than simply a volunteer who works with the less fortunate; she is a leader and an organizer who devotes her time encouraging others to get involved and then designs opportunities for them to do just that. After her summer of volunteer work at YUM, she planned and initiated a three-day service camp for Jakarta International School (JIS) students at the YUM Community Center in Cipanas, West Java. From the forty students who volunteered, sixteen were carefully chosen for this first service camp. Her goal was to get JIS students and YUM volunteers working more closely together.

Priscilla is also a realist and recognizes that young people in her school don't often see the physical reality of poverty "up close and in person." They may engage in fundraising to help disadvantaged children and their families, but they don't truly know those families and the reality of their lives. However, if they go to a place like YUM where they have a chance to work with needy children and get to know them, then she believes that kids from her school are much more likely to get involved—and stay involved. To give her JIS schoolmates an opportunity to be more connected, Priscilla organizes experiences like the YUM Service Camp.

Does it work? Listen to the words of one of the JIS students who attended the camp. "The three days that we spent away from the city was an unforgettable experience. It really opened our eyes to what was happening only two hours away from us. The YUM camp was something that none of us will ever forget, showing us a world we had never encountered before." That's precisely the kind of awareness Priscilla wants her classmates to have.

Making students and faculty more aware of the stark reality of conditions around them and convincing them to do something to improve those conditions can be a challenge, she explains, especially when both students and faculty live in the security and isolation of an international community. Speaking to an audience of 300 international school faculty members, Priscilla used the metaphor of a cruise ship (a metaphor she says her social studies teacher gave her) to describe that security and isolation. Like passengers on a luxury ship, she says, expats can cruise along in their self-contained world, oblivious to the lives of people in their host country—people who may be working for only three dollars a day.

That kind of "cruise ship obliviousness" is not just a loss for the people in the host country, but for expats as well, especially young people like her. Priscilla believes that getting involved in the community isn't just a decent thing to do; it's the essence of what it means to be a global citizen. The key is to not always orient your life to what is *good* for you, but be aware of what is going on around you and try to do what is good for *others*; that's the responsibility of a global citizen.

When expats connect with local people and develop relationships with them, it can be good for the locals, and it can also be useful for the expats as well, offering opportunities to learn about the local culture. And in the process of becoming involved with a new culture, expat kids can discover potential in themselves that they may not have recognized before. "I learned that I am good at dealing with people that I don't really know; I can be friendly and warm with them," Priscilla admits. She has also realized that she has the ability to step up and be a leader when it is clear that nobody seems ready to take the initiative, as she did in organizing the YUM Service Camp.

Priscilla Acuna Mena balks at the suggestion that she is a *natural* leader and organizer, but others clearly recognize that quality in her. When the Jakarta International School decided to reorganize its humanitarian service organization, *Help the Children, Tolong Anak Anak* (TAA), Priscilla was given the task of both explaining the reorganization and leading the new group.

It wasn't an easy task; some of those confronted with the reorganization referred to it as a "socialist takeover." So, one of Priscilla's first tasks was to refute this notion and explain how the reorganization made the groups in the new configuration more accountable and allowed people throughout the school to take the concept of community service more seriously.

As a leader in her school, Priscilla has also been involved in organizing activities for the Global Initiative Network in Indonesia, including a conference at JIS. She and a team of Jakarta International School (JIS) students completed a presentation at a recent Global Initiative Conference, taking other international school students through a process demonstrating how they can implement initiatives that address global problems at a local level.

The Global Initiative Network (GIN) is an idea inspired by Jean-Francois Rischard, former World Bank President for Europe. In his book *High Noon: Twenty Global Problems, Twenty Years to Solve Them* written in 2002, Rischard comments that existing institutions simply cannot react fast enough to deal effectively with recurring global challenges. He suggests the establishment of GINs made up of experts in various fields. Members of the networks would work both individually and collectively to come up with various strategies for dealing with these emerging challenges. Schools like Jakarta International School in the East Asia Council of Overseas Schools have taken Rischard's recommendation to heart and have established their own Global Initiative Network.

Priscilla is now a graduate of JIS and currently is attending Stanford University, but she has left behind leaders she has mentored to replace her and carry on the work she began at *Help the Children* (TAA) and YUM. Like other effective leaders, she knows the importance of passing on the leadership torch to the next generation. It is they who will ensure that the initiatives she has begun continue to thrive.

Like other young heroes, Priscilla has great faith in the ability of other young people to be positive agents of change. Her advice is, "Be persistent; even when you encounter hurdles and lack of support, keep your head up, keep going, because it's worth it." And she adds, "Find joy in the process of helping others since that is what is going to keep you motivated and keep you going." That joy in helping others is evident when she talks about her work. "It's reassuring to me that when I saw a need, I didn't just feel bad for a moment and then forget about it. I tried my best to do something at the level I could."

12.1: Priscilla in November 2014.

There is one more point about her work as a leader and organizer that Priscilla wants to share with other young leaders: It's one thing to be leading and organizing activities, but the important thing is that *you* are involved and active in doing those endeavors as well—working alongside the people you are trying to help. "It's not just, 'Hey look, I'm leading and organizing; I'm participating and doing things, too.' " In other words, a good leader must be actively working at the ground level as well.

Priscilla explains, "I think that getting involved in community service is just a decent thing to do. Also it is such a useful outlet for connecting with people from different backgrounds. Building these relationships helps uncover one of the fundamental truths of humanity: that we aren't all that different. If everyone understood this, I think the world would be a different place."

One of the ways she wants to make use of her learning is to help reduce the poverty and inequality she has seen in the world—reduce it not just in the short-term but also in the long-term. Not surprisingly, Priscilla remains highly involved in community service work in and around Stanford University. She is the Parent Engagement Coordinator at DreamCatchers Youth, an organization dedicated to supporting the education outcomes and health behaviors of low-income and minority youth. She volunteers as a Spanish interpreter at Cardinal Free Clinics operated by the Stanford School of Medicine that provides care for under-served or uninsured patients. She has also worked as a sexual assault counselor at a local rape crisis center, and is beginning to explore the role of political activism in effecting systemic change.

Priscilla Acuna Mena continues to embody her philosophy that young people can't wait for others to tackle the great social problems of their time. She also remains committed to the principle that one leads by example.

PART III

THE STUDENTS AND THEIR MENTORS

INTRODUCTION

Remember Mentor?

Do you remember Mentor from Greek Mythology? He was the trusted friend and teacher of Telemachus, Odysseus' son. When Odysseus went off to the Trojan War, he asked Mentor to look after his son. From time to time, Athena, the goddess of wisdom, disguised herself as Mentor and offered Telemachus guidance and encouragement from a feminine perspective. Thus, Telemachus received the benefits of both male and female mentoring.

Certainly none of the mentors in this book claim to be a goddess or god, but each in his or her own way has offered the wisdom, encouragement and support to the young person that he or she needed at critical times in order to accomplish what that young dreamer had set out to do. Without the assistance of mentors, our heroes would have found it much more difficult, and in some cases, impossible to achieve their goals.

Male or female, a mentor can be a parent or a teacher, a sibling or even a close friend. Yet, whatever the relationship, the mentor works behind the scene, encouraging, guiding, reassuring and at times reanimating the young hero to follow his or her dream. In no instance does the mentor attempt to usurp control of the hero's project. As mentors they recognize and accept their role as supporter and counselor (when needed), knowing that the young person must be the mover and the shaker who both initiates and completes the important task he or she has set out to accomplish.

Occasionally, it is something a mentor says that spurs a young hero to action, as when Dylan's mom made a comment about how the food he was wasting could feed an entire family living in poverty. Sometimes the mentor suggests an idea that captures the heroes' imagination and launches them on their quest. In this next section, you will read about Betsy Sawyer's comment that perhaps the Bookmakers and Dreamers Big Book project could be about world peace, and Jennifer Henbest de Calvillo's idea that her students could do something to address the emotional needs of children who were victims of the 2011 tsunami in Japan. In other cases, the hero herself sees a need that she wants to address and the mentor provides the assistance and support, keeping her energized and focused on her goal, as Peighton's father and Hannah's parents did.

Often the mentor also helps the young hero overcome an obstacle, or what in mythology is known as the threshold guardian—someone or something that stands in the way of the hero either initiating or completing his or her project. The most common threshold guardians that kids and teens encounter are actually adults who are simply skeptical about a student's ability to accomplish the goal he or she has in mind. In that case, the mentor is often helpful in getting the hero beyond this barrier either by providing useful advice or by being a visible presence beside his or her "mentee."

In the three chapters that follow, you will see the importance of mentors and appreciate how they work to support the efforts of our young heroes.

13

Children's Wishes for Japan

Art washes from the soul the dust of everyday life.
~ Pablo Picasso

"When the tsunami happened, we were on school break, but when we got back to school we were thinking about what we could do to help kids up in Tohoku. The disaster was so big and we wanted to do something just for the kids," explains Malka Bobrive, a second grader at Osaka International School of Kwansei Gakuin (OIS). The 2011 earthquake off the coast of Tohoku, Japan had just occurred that sparked a tsunami with waves as high as 40.5 meters (133 ft.) and resulted in massive destruction and hundreds of deaths.

Malka watched on television, with a mixture of awe and horror, the destruction that such a powerful act of nature produced. She was not the lone witness to those tragic events; millions of people of all ages around the world watched as that devastation, and the human misery that accompanied it unfolded.

Nor was eight-year-old Malka alone in her desire to do at least one small thing to relieve the misery of the children she knew had lost their homes, and in certain cases lost their parents and everything else they loved.

Anri Shingli Pok, (who at the time was a sixth grader) recalls, "I wanted to do something that would be special for an individual child who had lost everything." Their art teacher Mrs. Jennifer Henbest de Calvillo had a similar yearning as she watched the news coverage of the disaster. For three days she was distressed by the images of human misery that she witnessed on television. Like Malka and Anri, her thoughts turned especially toward the pain that the children must be experiencing. She too wanted to do something to ease their sadness. But do what?

Together with hundreds of others, Malka, Anri and their teacher Jennifer Henbest de Calvillo would find a way to address the emotional needs of children through a project they called Children's Wishes for Japan. The project would use the arts as a means to help heal the wounds of the Tohoku children who had suffered so much loss.

"I wanted to use art as healing," said Anri. So did her teacher and many other students at Osaka International School of Kwansie Gakuin. Thus began a project of designing beautifully artistic bags and filling them with art, music, and calligraphy (inkstones, ink and brush sets for Shodo [Japanese-style calligraphy] supplies. They also filled the bags with something else, something very special and very personal—words of support and encouragement from caring children around the world.

The project had a modest beginning, sparked by a donation of $100 dollars by Jennifer Henbest de Calvillo's father. But she and her young cohorts had a much bigger goal. They planned to raise at least $10,000 to send out hundreds of Children's Wishes bags to those who had lost so much. They would not be deterred.

13.1: Second grader, Malka Bobrive is holding the bag she painted.

Anri designed posters about the project to put up in her school; she also sent them via email to other Japanese schools and to international schools throughout the world. Mrs. Calvillo, who had worked in international schools in Myanmar, Zimbabwe, Thailand and Vietnam before coming to OIS, made contact with former colleagues and with friends she had made around the world. Malka and Anri began recruiting other OIS students and parents to help them with their project.

Working with their art teacher, Malka and Anri created a website that encouraged others to donate painted bags or money to buy art, calligraphy and music supplies to fill the bags. The website also encouraged children to write letters that would be included in the bags. "We ended up giving much more than a beautiful bag with art and music supplies," explains Malka. "We also included letters and drawings from kids around the world," drawings that could speak in any language without a translation.

One letter, typical of the thousands that were sent read:

Hello... many children like me are thinking about you from around the world. This is why we made this bag for you, so you can remember to be happy. We wish you the best in your recovery. Many kids like me are wishing you health and safety and renewed happiness.

The letters were included in the bags in their original written language, along with a Japanese translation.

Once completed, the bags were sent to students in Kirikiri Elementary School in Otsuchi Iwate Prefecture and to children of four other elementary schools in Japan that had been destroyed by the earthquake and the tsunami that followed. By the time the Children's Wishes for Japan project ended nine months after it had begun, over fifty schools in twenty different countries had made contributions, and $32,331 had been raised. More than 900 hand-painted bags had been sent to young people in grades kindergarten through twelve who were victims of the earthquake and its aftermath. Over two thousand letters accompanied those bags.

Most of us remember well the horror of the 2011 earthquake and tsunami in Japan. We recall that part of the

13.2: Anri working on her bag.

physical devastation produced by that earthquake and tsunami was the damage to the Fukishima Nuclear Power Plant and that, as a result of that damage, radioactive nuclear waste was released into the air, water and ground in Miyagi Prefecture—radioactivity that will make much of that area unlivable for hundreds of years. The physical loss and painful memories of people who lived through those tragic events will linger for many years—perhaps a lifetime—yet Malka and Anri realized that the healing could begin.

That is what Children's Wishes for Japan was all about, especially in relation to the children who suffered through the tragedy and those who witnessed it. The project was designed to establish a link so that children could help children in a very personal way. For, as was noted on the project's website, food, water and clothing are the basic needs that must be addressed quickly in the aftermath of a disaster. But after that essential help has been given, then what?

During that time, many people worldwide sent donations to organizations like the American Red Cross, UNICEF, Save the Children, and Doctors Without Borders that helped provide the food, water, clothing, shelter and medical care that are immediate needs. But we all know there are needs that extend beyond the basic necessities. Children had lost their homes, their schools, their pets and toys and, in some cases, even their parents, their relatives and their friends. They were sitting in a shelter feeling bewildered and alone. What could be done for them beyond what had already been done? Remember what Anri said? "I wanted to do something that would be special for an individual child who had lost everything. I wanted to use art as healing."

Anri and Malka, their teacher Mrs. Jennifer Henbest de Calvillo, as well as those who worked with them, believed then and still believe now that art has the power to heal, especially when you receive it from someone who genuinely cares.

Anri explains, "If I got one of the bags, my first thought would be that other people care about me and that there is meaning to life." And Malka tells us, "For a long time you can't do anything after a disaster. Art makes you feel different; it helps you express the joy and sorrow of it." And Mrs. Calvillo emphasizes, "Art can heal, and children's art, especially, is very powerful."

Children's Wishes for Japan helped many students who were dealing with feelings of loss, separation and perhaps even despair as a result of having been displaced by the earthquake and tsunami. But it did something else as well. It convinced the young people who witnessed the events, along with the adults who worked with them, that they, these kids could be a powerful positive influence on the lives of others regardless of their age. That is a legacy that will continue long after the memories of the tragedy have faded.

"Mrs. Calvillo helped me realize that even though I'm young, I can help people," insists Anri. "I've learned that I feel better when I can do something and this will have a lasting effect on me," reveals Malka. "This is one of the best things I've ever become involved in during my life," admits Jennifer Calvillo. "I will never forget Anri and Malka either—the maturity and concern they showed and the role models they were and are for others their age."

During those first few days of terrible distress as Jennifer Henbest de Calvillo watched the events of the earthquake, tsunami and nuclear meltdown unfold and wondered what she could do to relieve some of misery she was seeing, she recalls hearing a song by Mecedes Sosa, *"Yo Vengoa Ofrecer mi Corazon"* ("I Come to Offer My Heart").

> Who said that all is lost?
> I come to offer my heart.
> So much blood that the river took
> I come to offer my heart.

By the time she arrived back at Osaka International School of Kwansie Gakuin after that school break, she found

Malka and Anri and a whole lot of other young people both in her school and from around the world who, like her, were ready to reach out to children in distress and offer not only art, calligraphy and music supplies, but offer their hearts as well.

14

A Step Forward for Peace

Let there be peace on earth
And let it begin with me,
Let there be peace on earth
The peace that was meant to be
~ Vince Gill

Sometimes a significant accomplishment begins with a little dream. That's what happened in the case of The Big Book Pages for Peace project that began as an after-school program at Groton-Dunstable Middle School in Groton, Massachusetts. It resulted in a book that is twelve feet high and ten feet wide. No, that's not a misprint. The book is actually twelve by ten feet and weighs more than a ton.

In the beginning, the dream of the eight original fifth graders who comprised the Bookmakers and Dreamers Club, and their teacher, Betsy Sawyer, was modest—to publish a book of student writing. Then one day a few of the Bookmakers and Dreamers were skimming through a copy of the *Guinness Book of Records*, reading about the biggest hamburger in the world, the longest fingernails in the world and—the *smallest* book in the world. They decided to try to create the *biggest* book in the world. Now their dream was certainly getting bigger.

Yet as big as the physical size of the book they created is, its subject matter is even grander, addressing the question: How would you bring about world peace? Their Big Book Pages for Peace contains over 1,300 responses to that question and other questions related to world peace. Many of the poems, stories and wishes were written by young people from around the world; others were submitted by adults, including soldiers and First Responders to the 9/11 World Trade Center tragedy. Still more were replies from people whose names you would easily recognize: the Dali Lama, Jimmy Carter, Dr. Helen Caldicott, Ted Kennedy, Pete Seeger, the late Nelson Mandela and the late Maya Angelou.

The Big Book project generated a lot of enthusiasm and publicity worldwide as it was being created. In September 2008, the Bookmakers and Dreamers and their teacher, Betsy Sawyer, were invited to present their project's goal to the United Nations Youth Peace Conference in New York City. They have also been recognized for their contribution to the cause of world peace by John Feal, founder of the Feal-Good Foundation that provided assistance to those families affected by the 9/11 tragedy, and now provides support for the First Responders who were called to Ground Zero. And in 2010, the Bookmakers and Dreamers received the Children's Courage of Conscience Award from the Peace Abbey whose mission is to create innovative models for society that empower individuals on the paths of nonviolence, peacemaking, and cruelty-free living.

When this project was originally initiated in 2004, it did not begin with a grandiose dream of helping to bring about world peace, nor was there a stampede of students to join the Bookmakers and Dreamers Club. Amory Willcox, one of the original members who is now in college, had no particular reason for joining the group when she signed up. She certainly had no idea what its mission would evolve into. She says that she signed on simply because the writing group needed more people if it was to be approved as an afterschool activity by the school administration.

Even Betsy Sawyer had little understanding of what she was getting into. When the students took their idea about creating the biggest book in the world to her, she agreed, thinking that this was a far-fetched idea and they'd forget about it within a few weeks. But they didn't. After all, this was a group that had named its club Bookmakers and Dreamers. So clearly, it was not unusual for them to dream big, especially when the dream was about books.

In the beginning though, the club's members were not thinking about a book that would promote world peace; they were merely dreaming about creating a very BIG book. "We were talking about designing and writing a large poetry book or a vegetable story," explains Becky Glennie, another original member. "And then Mrs. Sawyer went to a Jimmy Cliff concert and came back all fired up about a question Cliff had asked, "What have you done to promote world peace lately?" Mrs. Sawyer's fire quickly ignited her students' enthusiasm and The Big Book Pages for Peace project was underway. An unassuming beginning had become a magnificent dream.

Once the project was underway, the club's challenges became even bigger. When you're putting together a 500-page book that is twelve feet long and twenty feet wide when opened, you are going to need some serious professional assistance. Where would you find paper strong enough that won't tear when you turn pages that are that big? Come to think of it, how will you turn the pages at all?

Creative students in the College of Engineering at the University of Massachusetts in Lowell helped the club solve those two problems. They ran a number of tests that determined DuPont's Tyvek was strong enough and yet light enough to be the practical choice for the pages. They also designed a model of a robotic page turner that would eventually be used for the book.

Yet, even with those two major challenges resolved, there still remained the problem of finding a printer who could and would take on a project of this size. A little research led the Bookmakers and Dreamers to EFI VUTEk in Meredith, New Hampshire, a company that manufactured grand format ink jet printers. The EFI VUTEk staff not only introduced the Bookmakers and Dreamers to UniGraphic, a printing company in Woburn, Massachusetts that agreed to print the book, but EFI VUTEk also donated the ink that would be required to produce the book.

Once the project was well on its way to completion, the middle school Bookmakers and Dreamers had time to reflect upon what they hoped to accomplish beyond getting their Big Book into the *Guinness Book of World Records*. None of the four students (of eight) interviewed were naïve enough to believe that a book about peace, no matter how large, could by itself, bring about world peace; yet student Erik McIntosh expressed a hope that all of them shared: "I don't think the book will be the cause of world peace, but I do hope that it will be an inspiration for people to try to create world peace."

In actuality, the Big Book Pages for Peace project has already inspired many people to work together to advance the goal of achieving world peace. In addition to the 1,300 individuals who contributed written responses for the book, there is also the connection that has been established with 9/11 First Responders through the Feal-Good Foundation, and the assistance the Bookmakers and Dreamers have gotten from University of Massachusetts engineering students, as well as the contributions the group has received from EFI VUTEk and from UniGraphic. And in June 2011, the town of Groton, home of the Bookmakers and Dreamers, was the site of a World Music for World Peace Festival.

Then there's this: At a time when newspapers and radio and television newscasts are saturating the public with one story after another about bullying in schools, the Big Book Pages for Peace project seems to have had a pacifying influence in its own school. While acknowledging that the school principal and school committee have a strong policy against bullying, the four students interviewed believe that their club, with its Pages for Peace project, has helped limit incidents of bullying in their school.

"I think that everyone has been impacted by our club in one way or another," explains Nick Marsh. "It definitely has been preventing people from being bullied. If someone is being harassed, somebody else who doesn't even know the two parties will step in and say, 'You've got to stop this.'" The parents who were present during the interview seemed to agree with Nick on this point.

The Big Book Pages for Peace project began with a small group of eight middle school students who had a big dream and an unshakeable confidence in their ability to make their dream a reality. It wasn't easy and they all acknowledge they couldn't have accomplished it by themselves. They have had the help of many other students who have since joined their writing group. They have also had the unstinting encouragement of an inspiring teacher, Betsy Sawyer, and have been supported by many adults and young people in their community and beyond. But in the end, it was their vision, their optimism, their determination, and their perseverance that brought the project to the point where it was realized. We should be inspired by these heroes as we pursue our own dream of eventually living in a peaceful world. The Big Book's website is http://www.pagesforpeace. org/home.html.

In their own words they explain:

"I think that if everyone has at least the basic well-being of everyone else in mind, and decides they are not going to use violence to solve their problems, that's the way to build world peace." Becky Glennie

"Keep difficult situations from reaching a violent state. Arguments and disagreements may be useful because they help people to understand one another. But try to make sure they don't escalate into something dangerous." Erik McIntosh

"Slow down and ask yourself what you really want. Do I really want world peace? Once everyone has that common goal, which is our [Bookmakers and Dreamers] goal and my personal goal, then I think it will happen. My favorite quote is by Leo Buscalia: "Too often we underestimate the power of a touch, a smile, a kind word, a listening ear, an honest compliment or the smallest act of caring—all of which have the potential to turn a life around." I think that says it all: If you do the smallest thing for someone, it will do so much more than you can ever imagine." Amory Willcox

Mahatma Gandhi proclaimed, "If we are to teach real peace in this world, and if we are to carry on a real war against war, we shall have to begin with the children." These are certainly wise words spoken by a wise man. The Big Book Pages for Peace project embodies this wisdom. Just as we celebrate the wisdom of Gandhi, a visionary hero, let's acknowledge and celebrate the wisdom and work of young people today, who not only have big dreams about a peaceful world, but are also working to make those dreams reality.

On June 2, 2012 members of the world community got a preview of the first 150 pages of The Big Book Pages for Peace that was displayed at a ceremony held in Groton, Massachusetts to honor its creators. The night before, two of those middle school students who had started the club with their teacher Betsy Sawyer graduated from high school. By then they knew that their book would not be recorded in the *Guinness Book of World Records* as the biggest book in the world. A group of businessmen from Dubai had paid three million dollars to have a book about the prophet Mohammed printed in Germany. Unfortunately, its overall dimensions were larger than the Big Book's.

However, that news has not dismayed the original eight members of the Bookmakers and Dreamers, nor the more than 180 students who have been part of the club since

14.1: The completed Big Book Pages for Peace in Boston in late 2014.

its inception ten years ago. They know that their dream of creating a big book devoted to establishing world peace has and will continue to inspire others for years to come.

The Big Book Pages for Peace is now 1,080 pages long. It was unveiled at a World Kick-Off Gala Dinner and Fundraiser at the John F. Kennedy Presidential Museum and Library in Boston, Massachusetts on October 8, 2014. The Big Book is scheduled to travel to museums around the world. Those pages will eventually be seen by millions of people who also dream of a peaceful world.

15

The Burrito Boyz

You must give something to your fellow man.
Even if it is a little thing,
do something for those who have need of help,
something for which you get no pay except the privilege of doing it.
~ Dr. Albert Schweitzer

Luke Trolinger admits that the first time he and his friend Alec went with Alec's parents Michael and Mehrnaz Johnson to distribute burritos to homeless people in San Diego, he was nervous and frightened. "At first, I stayed in the car and didn't interact with the homeless people at all. I'd never associated with the homeless before; I believed they were all smelly druggies and criminals."

That was 223 consecutive Sundays and 87,328 hot meals ago (as of February 8, 2015) and Luke has been an enthusiastic participant in that burrito making and distribution activity ever since. In fact, he is one of the original members of a group of seven boys known as The Burrito Boyz, whose story has been chronicled in local newspapers, and on the CBS Evening News, and were acknowledged by *People* magazine as Heroes Among Us in 2014. And what a story it is!

Feeding the homeless wasn't initially Luke or Alec's idea, even though it has now become their passion. The idea was hatched by Alec's parents after they read both Alec's and

Luke's Christmas wish lists mentioning things like iPods and cell phones. The Johnsons decided that the boys needed a reality check. They devised a plan that they hoped would give the boys a perspective on how fortunate they were compared to many other people. So on a Sunday morning, they asked Luke and Alec join them in the kitchen where they made fifty-four hot burritos.

When the cooking was completed, they all drove in the Johnson's car from their middle class residential neighborhood in Tierrasanta to downtown San Diego. They drove along looking for homeless people living on the streets and passed out the breakfast burritos to anyone they found. Then they parked outside a homeless shelter and began to hand out burritos to people who passed by. At first, as Luke has explained, it was Alec and his parents who were handing out the burritos since he was too nervous to even get out of the car. Sitting in the car watching them pass out breakfast to grateful recipients, Luke's impression of homeless people began to change. They were not smelly druggies and criminals; they were ordinary people who were not as fortunate as he and his friend. Before long, he was standing beside the Johnsons greeting people in need and handing them hot food and water bottles.

The very next weekend, they handmade another fifty-four breakfast burritos in the family kitchen—paid for out of their own pocket—and greeted the less fortunate on the downtown streets with the hot meal, a bottle of water and a touch of dignity. "It felt like punishment at first when my dad told me the idea," Alec says with a laugh. "But to see human beings sleeping on the cold ground outside, it really touched me," he says. "I realized how much they don't have and how much we do have. It's a huge part of my life now." Trolinger agrees. "We learned to see the person beneath the grit and the grime," he explains. "They're just ordinary people down on their luck."

The Johnsons hadn't planned on making and distributing burritos to the homeless a long-term activity; they figured that doing it for a couple of weeks would give the boys a new perspective. But a remarkable thing happened. The two boys began to look forward to the Sunday excursions and wanted to continue. "After two visits, I started to really enjoy the experience," explains Luke. Alec was clearly enjoying it, too. After the first couple of weeks, Michael Johnson says he knew the boys were hooked.

It didn't take long for Alec and Luke to connect with the homeless people they served every Sunday. They made friends with a number of those impoverished people. Their first friend was David, a wheelchair bound homeless man, who would eventually accompany the boys to one of their soccer games. Other friendships soon developed with Eddie, Blue, Cowboy, Flacko and Wild Bill.

In his "Day of Affirmation" speech delivered in June 1966, Robert Kennedy remarked: "Each time a man stands up for an ideal, or acts to improve the lot of others, or strikes out against injustice, he sends forth a tiny ripple of hope. Crossing each other from a million different centers of energy and daring, those ripples build a current that can sweep down the mightiest walls of oppression and resistance." Alec and Luke soon discovered just how right Kennedy was about tiny ripples building into strong currents.

First, five friends from their Quest soccer team joined them in passing out burritos on Sunday mornings. Then Mike May, a businessman, read about the boys in a local newspaper and offered to let them use the kitchen of his Long Island Mike's Pizzeria to make their burritos. Soon, instead of making fifty-four burritos a week, the seven boys were making 500 and feeding the growing number of homeless people who waited for them at the corner of 16th and Market Street, as well as at a second stop at 13th and K Streets. What had begun as a ripple was rapidly developing into a strong current and that current would soon grow even stronger.

As the momentum continued to build and the boys' commitment showed no signs of wavering, Michael Johnson helped the boys develop a website [still active] called Hunger2Help. That domain name was actually the original name of the group, but once the newspapers got hold of the boys' story, reporters began to refer to Alec and Luke and their friends as The Burrito Boyz and that name stuck. Their website, Kids Taking Action is at: http://hunger2help.com/.

When the CBS Evening News found out about the boys and their project and broadcast a segment about them, the current of support got even stronger. A growing cadre of parents began to accompany the boys on Sundays. Members of Girl Scout troop #5273 from Chula Vista (now fondly referred to as The Burrito Babes) volunteered to help and give the boys one Sunday a month off. The Hunger2Help website began to receive cash donations from as far away as England and Australia. As Alec Johnson points out, "People are just looking to help. Since they just can't fly over here [to the USA], they donate money online instead."

In the hope of expanding the repertoire of things they could offer to the homeless, the boys composed letters and sent them to the local Trader Joe's and other area stores asking for donations. The retailers responded by supplying not just

15.1: Burrito Boyz in April 2013 at a City Council meeting. (Front row, left to right) Michael Johnson, Cole Smith, Luke Trolinger, Justin McDonald, Jim McElroy. (Back row, left to right) Julian Wahl, Joe Skvarna, Alec Johnson, Nick Peeleman.

food and water, but other items as well. Now, The Burrito Boyz were providing the homeless with tarps, sweaters, toilet paper, books, toys for their children, and even dog food and dog biscuits for their pets. As Burrito Boy Joe Skvarna pointed out, some homeless people owned dogs before they became homeless and they kept their animals through their changing circumstances.

The Burrito Boyz see their mission as much more than simply bringing breakfast and other necessary supplies to the homeless; they intend to nourish the spirits of those people with hope and inspiration. They have specific expectations for those who help them serve the homeless:

- Make eye contact.

- Be kind.
- Ask people how they are doing.
- Ask for and use their name.

Justin McDonald, another Burrito Boy, expressed the long-term effect he believes their work will have. "I think what we do has a bigger impact on the homeless community than just giving them breakfast. When they see kids taking action, it may make them want to do something to get their life back on track."

Indeed, the Burrito Boyz' commitment to helping others has had a broader influence than just on the homeless community they serve. There are now at least twenty other groups who have dedicated themselves to helping the homeless throughout the United States since hearing about Hunger2Help.

But let's step back a bit. Do you remember how this initiative got started and what its original purpose was? So it's fair to ask the question: Has preparing a Sunday breakfast for homeless men, women and children changed the perspective of either Alec and Luke? Luke certainly recognizes a change in himself and told us, "This activity has really shaped my view on life. Now I take nothing for granted; I'm actually appreciating what I have for the first time. As teenagers, we ask for so much and the homeless ask for so little." Nick Peeleman, one of Alec's and Luke's Quest team members who joined The Burrito Boyz a few months after they began their work, reflected on the difference between the lives of the homeless and the lives of he and his friends: "They don't use computers, they don't use technology, they don't have books; homeless people

15.2: Burrito Boyz in late 2014. [From left to right]: Nick Peeleman, Justin McDonald, Alec Johnson, Luke Trolinger, Joe Skvarna, Julian Wahl and Cole Smith.

have minimal material things. It shows us how grateful we should be for what we have."

Being a Burrito Boy is a special honor. It isn't just something you are entitled to; it is something you have to earn by commitment to the mission of Hunger2Help and by regular attendance at the Sunday production and distribution service. And you have to be voted in by the current members. Yet, The Burrito Boyz isn't an exclusive club either; five new members have recently been added to the group, and current members have already made plans that will ensure that their siblings and friends will replace them and continue their work when they move on.

The once tiny ripple of hope for the homeless that began with Alec and Luke will continue to grow into a stronger and stronger current of support and encouragement even after the original Burrito Boyz have been replaced. That changing of the guard, however, is still quite a bit in the future; the original band of Burrito Boyz are now in their junior year of high school and don't plan on stopping until they head to college.

The Burrito Boyz have a piece of sound advice for all of us who want to make our world better. As one of them told us, "A lot of people *talk* about helping out in the community but it's only in taking *action* that you can change the world." Additionally, every one of The Burrito Boyz will tell you that helping those less fortunate than you doesn't just make others' lives better, it makes your life better, too.

There is a moving postscript to The Burrito Boyz story. Recall that it was Alec Johnson's father, Michael and his wife, Mehrnaz who got the boys started on the project that has changed their lives. It turns out this project changed Michael Johnson's life as well. In early 2014, inspired by his son's and his son's friends' passion for helping others, Michael changed jobs and went to work as Vice President for Development with the San Diego Rescue Mission, an organization dedicated to helping the homeless.

EPILOGUE

They Are Truly Heroes

Former Baltimore Colts kicker Jim O'Brien once observed, "The thing about Americans is that we have no heroes of substance, only athletes and movie stars." Most people would agree with O'Brien, although some might point out that he neglected to add pop singers to his short list of celebrated heroes. Americans, however, are by no means the only ones who have a hard time identifying and acclaiming heroes of substance. Pick almost any nationality and you will confront essentially the same problem. A major reason for this is that people often confuse celebrity status with heroism. Young people in particular may fall victim to this confusion because athletes, movie stars and pop singers are given constant media exposure.

But there are genuine heroes of substance in every society often flying under the radar of media exposure, and not just a few of them, as the stories in this book demonstrate, are young people whose commitment to helping others is awe inspiring. Fortunately, that commitment bodes well for the future of humanity.

As we mentioned in our introduction, *hero* means, "to serve and protect." To the Greeks, a hero was someone who willingly sacrificed his needs and comfort for the greater good of others. Empathy and self-sacrifice were defining characteristics of all heroes in ancient times, as they should be for us today. The young people whose philanthropic work is recorded here certainly possess those qualities, in addition to persistence, perseverance and commitment.

Like the seeker mentioned at the beginning of this book, these youngsters have heard a voice deep down inside them that told them they were made to do something about the misery they have witnessed. They have responded to that voice, and they and our world are better as a result.

One final thought. The young heroes whose stories you have just read are not content to battle singlehandedly the misfortune and sorrow they see around them. They want an army of courageous young people, as determined as they are, to join them in the work of eliminating human suffering and hardship. They want many others, the young as well as the mature, to work with them to make the world a better place in which all of us can live happily. *Are you ready to join them?*

APPENDIX I

key themes

The kids and teens we interviewed for this book:

- Recognize they are fortunate and that there are many others who are far less fortunate. They hope to change the fortunes of those less fortunate.

- Strive for long-term sustainable outcomes with the projects they have initiated.

- Advise other young people to get involved in helping to make the world better.

- Developed over time, through persistence, the skills and abilities to bring their projects to fruition.

- Recognize that before long they will be the adults who will be assuming responsibility for leadership in the world and have decided to assume responsibility for providing some of that leadership right now.

- Strongly believe that they benefit as much from helping others as those they help.

APPENDIX II

What Adults Can Do to Encourage Young People

We began this book with John Gardner's observation, "One of the most difficult problems we face is to make it possible for young people to participate in the great tasks of their time ... We have designed our society in such a way that most possibilities open to the young today are either bookish or frivolous." There is nothing that compels us to maintain that design and there are very good reasons for us to change it.

As mentioned before in Chapter 12, Jean-Francois Rischard identified a variety of challenges that urgently demanded, but have, so far, eluded humanity's ability to solve them. His list, similar to the United Nations Millennium Development Goals, includes global warming, deforestation, elimination of poverty, conflict prevention, providing education for all, and elimination of water deficits. Among the obstacles he cited for getting these problems solved expeditiously was an aging population in many countries. This reality speaks directly to the need for engaging young people in tackling these great problems of our times.

Rischard suggested one approach for engaging people of all ages in embarking upon global problems. He proposed establishing Global Issues Networks [GINS] in which both professionals and non-professionals in various fields discuss methods to address these challenges. A number of schools have taken Rischard's suggestion and developed their own GINS. The stated mission of these particular schools that run GINS is to encourage and assist young people to work locally, regionally and internationally to address the world's problems. As you have discovered, certain young people have, on their own, taken the initiative to establish international networks via the Internet for their projects.

Even so, adults can inspire and support a young person's desire to make the world a better place in which to live. To inspire literally means, "to breathe spirit or life into something." Jennifer Henbest de Calvillo undertook that when her students expressed a desire to do some small thing to ease the pain of children who had lost so much in the Japanese earthquake and tsunami. Betsy Sawyer did too, with her students' desire to create a big book that would be included in the *Guinness Book of World Records*.

Indeed, a person in an administrative position can also be a source of inspiration for a young potential hero even as he or she performs his or her vital role as threshold guardian. As you remember, JinJin Xu's principal Ed Ladd acknowledged that he was a bit doubtful about her EggsChange proposal when she first approached him with it. "My first reaction was that this was a far flung idea from an idealistic freshman who had no idea how difficult this project would be to pull off."

Instead of dismissing her proposal as impractical, however, Ladd asked a lot of questions, a number of which JinJin had never considered. However, rather than being discouraged, she went home and drew up a full-scale business plan that addressed his questions. When she returned with that plan, he was so impressed he became determined to support her.

Yet, encouragement for a potential young hero doesn't demand that an adult immediately jump up and shout, "You can do it; go for it." Krithika Mahalingam admits that when her son Dylan first expressed an interest in starting a project to help victims of hunger, she was skeptical. "I didn't know if he wanted to do this because he really liked the cause or whether he just wanted to stay up late and SKYPE with somebody in Australia or the Netherlands since, 'that was really cool.'"

What we have found is that it's important for an adult who may be unsure about a young person's commitment to an activity to refrain from discouraging the young dreamer and actually give them an opportunity to show their perseverance and conviction.

Here are a few suggestions for adults who wish to support a potential young hero who has a philanthropic project in mind:

- Show that you have faith in the potential and integrity of young people in general and in particular, the young person you hope to encourage and support.

- Never just dismiss an ambitious project proposed by a young person, yet don't be shy about asking probing questions that ensure they have carefully considered all the challenges they might face when they undertake the project.

- Be prepared to give advice or assistance if a youngster or adolescent asks for it, but never lose sight of the fact that this is *their* project. Don't let it become your project instead of theirs. Peighton's Dad helped her compose an appeal letter for collecting food items from her neighborhood, but he didn't write it for her.

- Be ready to help the young person find critical resources if he or she needs help locating them. Be there to provide encouragement at times when a young dreamer faces daunting obstacles (as she/he inevitably will) and worries that he/she will not succeed or be taken seriously.

- Model in your own life a commitment to helping others. All of our young heroes had teachers, parents, siblings, friends or other role models whose commitment to helping others inspired them to do likewise.

Every one of the young people mentioned in this book had at least one person, older and wiser, who helped them achieve their heroic goal. And each kid and teen can readily identify those supportive individuals. They all acknowledged that without the support of these teachers, siblings and friends, their project probably would have faltered—perhaps even failed.

Many more young people are waiting to become engaged in taking on the great challenges of our times and they have a lot to offer. The problems we now face at the beginning of the 21st century are numerous and formidable, and as Jean-Francois Rischard has pointed out, it is "high noon."

As adults, we can't afford to pull a Gary Cooper and try to tackle these challenges alone. It is imperative that we get young people involved. We must be prepared to be the Obi Wan Kenobi voice behind them that whispers, "May the Force be with you."

SELECTED BIBLIOGRAPHY

Gardner, J. W. (1995). *Self-Renewal: The Individual and the Innovative Society*. New York: W.W. Norton and Company.

Kennedy, R. (June 6, 1966). "Day of Affirmation Speech." *http://www.americanrhetoric.com/speeches/rfkcapetown.htm*

Rischard, J. F. (2002). *High Noon: Twenty Global Problems, Twenty Years to Solve Them*. New York: Basic Books.

Sacks, O. (1973, 1999). *Awakenings*. New York: Vintage Books, Division of Random House.

Schumacher, E. F. (1973). *Small Is Beautiful: Economics as if People Mattered*. New York: Harper & Row.

Seuss, D. (1971). *The Lorax*. New York: Random House.

ACKNOWLEDGEMENTS

Writing a book and preparing it for publication can be a daunting task that is seldom accomplished without the loving support and help of a number of individuals. This book is no exception. We wish to thank the many people who helped us locate the youngsters whose stories we tell in this book.

Principal Ed Kidd, formerly of Shanghai American School, is currently serving as Headmaster of Ridley College in Ontario, Canada; Deidre Fischer, formerly Head of Cebu International School, the Philippines is now Educational Consultant for DF Education Play Ltd. in Adelaide, Australia; Principal Craig Rodgers of Beijing City International School; Tim Carr, Head of Jakarta International School, as well as Patricia "Trish" Davies, formerly the school's Service Learning Coordinator and now a Government Administration Professional in Auckland, New Zealand; Alicia Lewis and Principal Brad Latzke of Shanghai American School (Puxi Campus); Jan Deleault, Counseling Dept. Head at Pinkerton Academy in New Hampshire; Principal R. Lance Potter formerly of Chiang Mai International School is currently an Assistant Professor and Director of the Educational Leadership Program at Eastern Washington University; the late Charles Barton, former Head of Saigon South International School; and Bill Oldread, Asst. Director of the East Asia Council of Overseas Schools [EARCOS].

We are very grateful to our daughter Amber Goolbis and daughter-in-law Stacy Larsen who spent many hours reading the manuscript and offering suggestions on the initial drafts of the chapters in this book. Additionally, there are no words that can adequately express the depth of our appreciation for Rabia Tredeau and the staff at Kalindi Press who worked tirelessly to prepare this book for publication.

In conclusion, we also wish to thank parents and teachers who have been so supportive in allowing us to conduct our interviews and who have provided additional background information about the remarkable young people in this book. Indeed, we owe the parents of our heroes very special thanks for their incredible assistance in terms of supplying photos, captions, current updates and so much more over these past several years during which we worked to bring this book to publication.

As with any project that involves as many people as this one, we run the risk of overlooking the contribution of someone without whose help the publication of this book would not have been possible. To those people, anonymous though they may be, we say thank you.

PHOTO CREDITS

1.1 [Chapter 1, photo 1], 1.2 and 1.3: All three photos taken by Peighton's father, Josh Jones.

2.1 and 2.2: Photos taken by Timmy "Mini's" mother, Tina Tyrrell.

2.3: Photo taken by Hannah Coltrain.

3.1 and 3.2: Both photos taken by Dylan's mother, Krithika Mahalingam Photography, *mahalphoto.com*.

4.1: Photographer unknown.

4.2: Photo taken by Brad Riew.

5.1 and 5.2: Photos taken by Samantha's mother, Giselle Fernandez.

5.3: Photo taken by Alejandro Trujillo.

6.1 and 6.2: Both photos taken by JinJin's father, Xu Xiao Ping.

7.1: Photo taken by Emily Shandorf.

7.2: Photographer unknown; photo provided by East Meets West Foundation (now called Thrive Networks).

8.1 and 8.2: Both photos taken by Kelly Perry.

8.3: Photo taken by John Morelos.

9.1: Photo taken by Mik Bjorkenstam.

9.2: Photo taken by David J. Turner.

10.1: Photo taken by Daniel Huang.

10.2 and 10.3: Both photos taken by Daniel's father, Hui Huang.

11.1: School photo; photographer unknown.

11.2: Photo taken by the event organizers, Songshuhui-Association of Science Communicators, *guokr.com* and Intel Inc., for the Intel Social Innovation Week TED talk.

12.1: Photo taken by Andrea Salazar.

13.1 and 13.2: Both photos taken by art teacher Jennifer Henbest de Calvillo.

14.1: Photo taken by Karen Riggert.

15.1 and 15.2: Both photos taken by Linda Brubaker.

About The Authors: Photo taken at Airlie Gardens in Wilmington, NC in April 2014 by Samuel J. Patton, a videographer and photographer, Springtide Productions, Madbury, NH.

OTHER TITLES OF INTEREST FROM HOHM PRESS / KALINDI PRESS

FREE RANGE LEARNING
How Homeschooling Changes Everything
by Laura Grace Weldon

Free Range Learning presents eye-opening data about the meaning and importance of natural learning. This information—from neurologists, child development specialists, anthropologists, educators, historians and business innovators—turns many current assumptions about school-based education upside down. The book's factual approach is balanced by quotes and stories from over 100 homeschoolers from the U.S., Canada, Germany, Australia, Ireland, New Zealand, Mexico, India and Singapore.

This book will also encourage and excite those parents who want their children to have the benefits, yet are also timid in approaching homeschooling. This is the only book anyone needs to make the choice and start the process of homeschooling children. It is applicable for young people from pre-school through high school.

Hohm Press: Paper, 312 pages, 50 b&w photos, $24.95
ISBN: 978-1-935387-09-1

CONSCIOUS PARENTING
Revised Edition with New Material
by Lee Lozowick

Any individual who cares for children needs to attend to the essential message of this book: that the first two years are the most crucial time in a child's education and development, and that children learn to be healthy and "whole" by living with healthy, whole adults.

Conscious Parenting offers practical guidance and help for anyone who wishes to bring greater consciousness to every aspect of childraising, including: * conception, pregnancy and birth * emotional development * language usage * the mother's and the father's role * the exposure to various influences * establishing workable boundaries * the choices we make on behalf on our children's education ... and much more.

Hohm Press: Paper, 336 pages, $19.95   ISBN: 978-1-935387-17-9

To Order: 800-381-2700, or visit our website, www.hohmpress.com

PARENTING, A SACRED TASK
10 Basics of Conscious Childraising
by Karuna Fedorschak

Moving beyond our own self-centered focus and into the realm of generosity and expansive love is the core of spiritual practice. This book can help us to make that move. It highlights ten basic elements that every parent can use to meet the everyday demands of childraising. Turning that natural duty into a sacred task is what this book is about. Topics include: love, attention, boundaries, food, touch, help and humor.

"There is no more rigorous path to spiritual development than that of being a parent. Thank you to Karuna Fedorschak for reminding us that parenting *is* a sacred task."
– Peggy O'Mara, Editor and Publisher, *Mothering Magazine.*

Hohm Press: Paper, 160 pages, $12.95   ISBN: 978-1-890772-30-7

TO TOUCH IS TO LIVE
The Need for Genuine Affection in an Impersonal World
by Mariana Caplan, Ph.D.
Foreword by Ashley Montagu

The vastly impersonal nature of contemporary culture, supported by massive child abuse and neglect, and reinforced by growing techno-fascination are robbing us of our humanity. The author takes issue with the trends of the day that are mostly overlooked as being "progressive" or harmless, showing how these trends are actually undermining genuine affection and love. This uncompromising and inspiring work offers positive solutions for countering the effects of the growing depersonalization of our times.

"An important book that brings to the forefront the fundamentals of a healthy world. We must all touch more."
– Patch Adams, M.D.

Hohm Press: Paper, 272 pages, $19.95   ISBN: 978-1-890772-24-6

To Order: 800-381-2700, or visit our website, www.hohmpress.com

YOU DON'T KNOW ANYTHING . . . !
A Manual for Parenting Your Teenagers
by Nadir Baksh, Psy.D. and Laurie Murphy, R.N., Ph.D.

This book offers immediate and clear help to parents, family members and teachers who are angry, confused, frustrated, sad, or at their wit's end in dealing with their teenagers. Beyond advice for crisis situations, *You Don't Know Anything . . .!* informs parents of the new stresses their kids today must cope with, suggesting ways to minimize these pressures for both adults and teens.

Patience, caring, vigilance, "street smarts," knowledge of the teenage brain – these are among the many skills that today's parent needs. The book points the way to those skills, and encourages parents and other adults to resume their legitimate roles in teenagers' lives.

Hohm Press: Paper; 188 pages, $12.95   ISBN: 978-1-890772-82-6

8 STRATEGIES FOR SUCCESFUL STEP-PARENTING
by Nadir Baksh, Psy. D. and Laurie Elizabeth Murphy, R.N., Ph.D.

No matter who you are, and how much experience you've had with kids, becoming a step-parent, and "blending" families is difficult work. This book presents eight strategies, in the form of action steps, to maximize anyone's chances of success in this endeavor. Written in a non-apologetic voice, *8 Strategies For Successful Step-Parenting* offers strong and specific direction to address current problems. Vignettes of thirty real-life family situations support the approaches suggested. Issues and examples are applicable cross-culturally, addressing the needs of both men and women.

Hohm Press: Paper, 188 pages, $14.95   ISBN: 978-1-935387-08-4

ABOUT THE AUTHORS

Mike Connolly worked as a high school, middle school and upper elementary school principal in urban, suburban and rural school districts in the United States before going abroad to work in prestigious international schools in Thailand, Costa Rica, the Netherlands and Vietnam. During his tenure as a principal, Mike offered workshops, seminars and classes at K-12 schools and universities, while also presenting at national and international conferences in London, Thailand, Malaysia and the USA.

In 2007, Mike retired after forty-two years in education to pursue his passion for writing and is the author of two books *What They Never Told Me in Principals' School* (2009) and *Teaching Kids to Love Learning, Not Just Endure It* (2011) published by Rowman and Littlefield. His articles have appeared in numerous national and international journals.

Mike and two of his former classmates are currently working on a book that chronicles how their four years in high school in preparatory seminary positively influenced the direction of their lives, even though none of them were ever ordained as priests.

Brie Goolbis served for twelve years as a school counselor in the United States. Later she worked as a college counselor, Dean of Students, Director of Counseling, as well as an Admissions and Marketing Director at prestigious international schools in four different countries on three continents. Her volunteer work has included administering the GED to high school dropouts in the state of New Hampshire, serving as a court mediator for families with children experiencing difficulties, and most recently as a Resource Volunteer for the American Cancer Society.

Brie's interests include yoga and vegetarian cooking. Most of all, she loves to reuse, repurpose, and recycle. Brie and Mike have been married for twenty-five years and have raised four children. They currently live in Hampstead, North Carolina.

ABOUT KALINDI PRESS

KALINDI PRESS, an affiliate of HOHM PRESS, proudly offers books in natural health and nutrition, those that promote self-responsibility, as well as the acclaimed *Family Health* and *World Health Series* for children and parents, covering such themes as nutrition, dental health, breastfeeding, early reading, and environmental education.

CONTACT INFORMATION

Hohm Press / Kalindi Press, PO Box 4410, Chino Valley, Arizona, 86323, USA; 800-381-2700, or 928-636-3331; *hppublisher@cableone.net*

Visit our website at: *www.kalindipress.com*